Advanced Placement Poetry

John Manear

The Center for Learning

John Manear, Center for Learning English consultant, teacher, and co-author of *AP English: In-depth Analysis of Literary Forms*, earned his M.A. at the University of Pittsburgh, PA. An English department chairperson currently serving as president of the Western Pennsylvania Council of Teachers of English, he has taught AP English for many years and conducted workshops for other AP teachers.

The Publishing Team

Rose Schaffer, M.A., President/Chief Executive Officer
Bernadette Vetter, M.A., Vice President
Diane Podnar, M.S., Managing Editor
Mary Anne Kovacs, M.A., English Consultant

Cover Design

Mary Kaperick

List of credits found on Acknowledgments Page beginning on 243.

ISBN 1-56077-379-0

Contents

Introduction

The following materials and exercises for teachers and students have been designed according to several assumptions about gifted students and Advanced Placement or Honors English classes.

Teaching the talented can be a delight. It can also be a difficult challenge! No less than their peers, highly capable students tire of strictly read-discuss-write academic programs. At the same time, they often reject the too-cute. They can, however, thrive on a varied, intellectually stimulating program geared toward developing their powers of analysis and synthesis to the highest possible level. The universal concerns of literature also contribute to the growth of empathetic hearts and keen minds.

The purpose of the AP program is to provide talented high school seniors with college-level courses. The AP examinations given in May of each year provided a standardized method of evaluating students' achievements and reporting them to colleges. The AP test includes both objective and essay sections, and it changes from year to year, always challenging students' ability to read prose and poetry. The exam stresses analytic skills, ability to synthesize, ability to think on their feet, and composition skills.

Advanced Placement and Honors classes generally consist of talented and highly motivated students. For many the goal is a high score in the AP exam, enabling them to test out of the freshman college English courses. Others are more interested in the experience of a high-powered English study or of being in class with others who are also serious about learning. Regardless of these varying short-term goals, the teacher can successfully help all students by providing a stimulating atmosphere through activities that challenge students' logic, creativity, insight, and technical skills. Most effective AP programs focus primarily on developing these abilities, rather than attempting to "teach to" the AP exam itself.

The materials in this unit are designed to help teachers incorporate extra challenge and enjoyment into AP, Honors, and Gifted English classes.

The focus, poetry, is an essential emphasis which must be incorporated into any Advanced Placement English curriculum. The end-of-the-year examination, with half of the objective section and one third of the essay section devoted to poetry, reflects that "need". Apart from the test itself, understanding and appreciation of all literary discourse results from the formation of a "poetics" in the Aristotle sense. An understanding of poetic discourse is an understanding of the "prime matter" out of which all literary expression evolves. The conventions of the short story, the novel, and the drama may vary, but their status as art or literary forms is a poetic consideration.

Since students are often distracted by the generic characteristics of other literary forms (the "story" element, for example), they are frequently disoriented when confronted with minimalistic or expressionistic examples of art. They tend to reject what they do not immediately understand

and to reject poetry that does not provide a ready and real narrative and message. Advanced Placement students are quite capable of becoming engaged in the subtleties and satisfactions that pure poetry can provide. However, they must be systematically exposed to its perfection. "Tell all the truth/But tell it slant." This unit is an effort to provide a systematic and integrated approach for such students.

Preliminary Notes
to the Teacher

Using the Course Materials

This book consists of teacher plans and student handouts for thirty-four lessons. The lessons included reflect only the special challenge objectives of an AP or Honors course. More basic educational approaches to the genres, composition, and major literary traditions are available through a variety of other Center for Learning texts.

Each lesson is designed for a tightly-compressed class period, including effective preliminary and follow-up work. Many lessons lend themselves to expansion to two or three class days. The handouts, numbered for quick reference, are intended for distribution to students. Students will need to keep handouts in an organized notebook or folder for use during succeeding lessons.

This unit is divided into four sections:

Part I, "The Formation of a Poetics," is a systemic presentation of the theoretical basis of poetic discourse, providing guidelines for analysis of poetic language in general (in contrast to "grammatical" and "rhetorical" discourse), as well as consideration of specific pieces of writing which we label "poems."

Part II, "The Naming of Parts," focuses on the various "parts" of a poem and attempts to strengthen the interactive alliance between the reader and the text.

Part III, "What Are Patterns For?," examines the varieties of patterns that are either imposed on or emerge from parts of or the total poem, "the best words in the best places."

Part IV, "Critical Perspectives," encourages and directs students to expand their own experiences of poetry through the selective reading of literary criticism. Students are also encouraged to evaluate their own critical position in the context of various schools of critical theory and to synthesize their study in a research assignment.

Teaching Approaches

Because peer group interaction is important in the learning process, many activities in this unit can involve students working with each other to fulfill specific goals. Because AP classes are often rather small and students frequently have come to know one another very well, it is helpful to allow flexibility in group formation rather than assigning regular partners or small groups.

Evaluation

Evaluation of student achievement in the AP course can be accomplished in several ways. Individual handouts provide daily means of checking on students' progress. Critical essays and discussions help to gauge students' growth in analysis and composition skills. While results of the May AP exam are not available until midsummer, too late for end-of-the-year grading, they are an invaluable tool for evaluating both individual students and the program itself.

Part I
The Formation of a Poetics

Introduction

Most students eventually conclude that what we call "literature" in an academic context has "value." They usually agree that they enjoy reading some short stories, novels, and plays, although uninitiated readers often resent the investment of time that such activity demands of them. Beyond enjoyment, they may see value in the philosophical, sociological, or even ethical dimensions of the work. Some even value various aesthetic qualities, admiring the author's ability to tell a story well, develop a lifelike character, or treat an enduring theme in a fresh and original way. But many students are at a loss for words when asked to articulate what, if anything, they see as the "value of poetry." Some may claim to "like" it in some vague way (although many will readily admit to a distaste for it), but they are usually unable to explain *why* in specific ways.

Most students can only differentiate between prose and poetry in terms of the "techniques" which they associate with each. It is still an established misconception, even among educated adults, to think of poetry in terms of verse (with rhyme and meter). Most students have similar expectations, usually based on their early experience of what they were told was poetry. That introductory experience may have generated a positive response on the part of a student. However, when later exposure to the wide range of poetic expression results in an encounter with poetry that is less narrative and more lyrical, less structured and more informal, confusion and bewilderment ensue. The student, seeing the "new poetry" as a violation of previously formulated aesthetics, may reject it. The consequent lack of effort to accept this new body of poetry on its own terms often results in a distaste for poetry which seems to be characteristic of even gifted students. Consequently, to reeducate these students, a systematic presentation of the theoretical basis of poetic discourse is helpful.

Lessons 1–9 attempt to guide the student through a variety of theoretical considerations which are inherent to the study of poetry. They presuppose a knowledge of most of the traditional techniques associated with poetic discourse. Therefore, some lessons function as a review. More to the point, they pose questions which are central to the formation of a theory of poetry, a poetics:

- What is poetry?
- What similarities and differences exist between poetic discourse and other modes?
- What does the poem itself tell us about the process which produced it?
- What does the poet, the practitioner, tell us about the poetic process?
- What function does the poem itself serve?

In general, then, the questions must be asked: Who, Why, When, What, How, and Where is poetry? Answers, of course, will be as diverse as the poets, poems, and people who participate in the various stages of the process.

Lesson 1
Prose and Poetry: Which Is "Best"?

Objectives

- To enable students to differentiate between the purposes which can be served by prose and poetry
- To test Samuel Taylor Coleridge's distinction: "Prose is words in their best order; poetry, the best words in the best order" (from *Table Talk*).

Notes to the Teacher

In order to establish a new way of thinking about poetry, students may need to air some of their discontentment with it. The following activities provoke some preliminary discussions of how poetry and prose differ in terms of both purpose and audience, differences that decidedly influence an author's "voice," selection of detail, and choice of words.

Procedure

1. Distribute **Handout 1,** which includes three poems based on an actual occurrence (as revealed in the journalistic account). Read the three poems and the news account with the students, and use them as the basis for a discussion of the "truth" of poetry and the "truth" of prose. Students will undoubtedly touch on such issues as emotional impact, editorializing, selection and organization of detail, and even tone. Allow the discussion to move in any of these directions, but continue to bring it back to the question of similarities and differences in the processing of information through prose and poetry.

2. Read Frost's poem "Out, Out—," **Handout 2,** with the students. Indicate that this poem was written in response to a newspaper account. Discuss how this poem differs from the three poems dealing with the death of Norman Morrison. Point out that Frost's poem is in response to the death of anyone so young, more than to a particular journalistic "event." As a result, the boy is not named nor are any but the most essential biographical details provided. Frost is more concerned with the dramatic reenactment of the moment in combination with the levels of response which it provokes in the narrator, the boy himself, his family, and, ultimately, the reader.

The poems concerning Norman Morrison, however, focus more on the degree to which society reacts or fails to react to a death which has a symbolic connection with the Vietnam War. Frost distances himself from his information in order to interpret its universal, emotional significance, while the other three poems focus on specific information in order to interpret its specific emotional significance.

3. If time permits following this discussion, have students formalize some of their responses by completing **Handout 3.** Otherwise, students may complete the handout as a homework assignment.

Suggested responses:

Part I

1. *Adrian Mitchell's poem provides the most factual information (date, place, means and motive for death, age, religious background, family members present). David Ferguson indicates only that Morrison "cradled" his infant daughter and "spoke in a tongue of flame near the Pentagon." It is assumed that his speech was in "silence" or in ritual as suggested by Starbuck's poem (which also reveals that Morrison was from Baltimore and that he, "while burning, screamed.").*

2. *There are multiple examples of the poets' editorial responses. For example:*
   a. *Ferguson implies that "the Pentagon . . . had no doubt" that the war was justified.*
   b. *Mitchell formulates Morrison's motivation in terms of a parallel:*

"He did it in Washington where
everyone could see
because
people were being set on fire
in the dark corners of Vietnam
where nobody could see."

  c. Starbuck draws a parallel between Morrison burning himself
and Robert McNamara, the Secretary of Defense, burning "a con-
centration of the Enemy Aggres-
sor."

3. Some of many examples of details include:

  a. Ferguson:
"spoke in a tongue of flame": his
action was a way of speaking; an
allusion perhaps to the Pentecos-
tal flame of the Holy Spirit (in Acts
of the Apostles, *New Testament*)
which inspired the disciples to
speak in tongues to the whole
world

  b. Mitchell:
"in the white heart of Washington": white, associated with purity, is used ironically
"put on a new skin of flame and
became Vietnamese": he becomes "the enemy" by dying as
they are dying

  c. Starbuck:
"burned/What he said was himself": implies that his "true self"
was not his body

Part II

1. Answers will vary but will contain
references to the following:

Who?   young boy/witnessed by
           sister/doctor called
Where? perhaps Vermont or near-
           by Massachusetts
How?   buzz-saw—died later un-
           der ether
When?   a late afternoon
Why?   accident

2. a. Answers will vary. Most students
will admit that their account does
not capture the emotion of the situation nor the philosophical comments of the narrator.

  b. Answers will vary. Some may
touch upon
sound effects: "buzz-saw snarled
and rattled"
precision: "then the boy saw all"
personification: " . . . the saw,/
As if to prove saws knew what
supper meant,/Leaped out at the
boy's hand . . ."

  c. ll. 4–6: "those that lifted" could
see the sunset far away,
foreshadowing the end of
the day and the end of
life.

    ll. 10–12: If they had called it a
day a half hour earli-
er, the boy would have
been pleased and
"saved" from both
work and death.

    ll. 33–34: Almost with cold-
blooded indifference
the narrator delivers
the poem from pathos.
There is no more to
build on after death
takes away life. The
turning to other af-
fairs is necessary. It is
the abruptness, with-
out warning or
mourning, that makes
the statement so star-
tling.

Name _____

Date _____

Poetic Perspectives

Norman Morrison

On November 2nd 1965
in the multi-coloured multi-minded
United beautiful States of terrible America
Norman Morrison set himself on fire
outside the Pentagon.
He was thirty-one, he was a Quaker,
and his wife (seen weeping in the newsreels)
and his three children
survive him as best they can.
He did it in Washington where everyone could see
because
people were being set on fire
in the dark corners of Vietnam where nobody could see.
Their names, ages, beliefs and loves
are not recorded.
This is what Norman Morrison did.
He poured petrol over himself.
He burned. He suffered.
He died.
That is what he did
in the white heart of Washington
where everyone could see.
He simply burned away his clothes,
his passport, his pink-tinted skin,
put on a new skin of flame
and became
Vietnamese.

—Adrian Mitchell

Norman Morrison

Not an unhappy man
but one who could not stand
in the silence of his mind
the cathedral
emptied of its ritual
and sounding about his ears
like a whirlwind.

He cradled the child awhile
then set her down nearby
and spoke in a tongue of flame
near the Pentagon
where they had no doubt.

    Other people's pain
    can turn so easily
    into a kind of play.
    There's beauty
    in the accurate
    trajectory. Death
    conscripts the mind
    with its mysterious
    precision.

—David Ferguson

Of Late

"Stephen Smith, University of Iowa sophomore, burned what he
                said was his draft card"
and Norman Morrison, Quaker, of Baltimore Maryland, burned
                what he said was himself.
You Robert McNamara, burned what you said was a
                concentration of the Enemy Aggressor.
No news medium troubled to put it in quotes.

And Norman Morrison, Quaker, of Baltimore Maryland, burned
                what he said was himself.
He said it with simple materials such as would be found in your
                kitchen.
In your office you were informed.
Reporters got cracking frantically on the mental disturbance
                angle.

So far nothing turns up.
Norman Morrison, Quaker, of Baltimore Maryland, burned and
                while burning, screamed.
No tip-off. No release.
Nothing to quote, to manage to put in quotes.
Pity the unaccustomed hesitance of the newspaper editorialists.
Pity the press photographers, not called.

Norman Morrison, Quaker, of Baltimore Maryland, burned and
                was burned and said
all that there is to say in that language.
Twice what is said in yours.
It is a strange sect, Mr. McNamara, under advice to try
the whole of a thought in silence, and to oneself.

—George Starbuck

7

The Pacifists

At 5:15 one afternoon last week, Norman Morrison, 31, his clothing doused in kerosene and his youngest child, 18-month-old Emily, cradled in his arms, stood outside the river entrance to the Pentagon and burned himself to death. As hundreds of departing officers and civilian workers watched—no photographers were on the scene—Army Major Richard Lundquist grabbed the child away from the flames. Army Lieutenant Colonel Charles Johnson, who had seen two Buddhists incinerate themselves on the streets of Saigon, and two Air Force sergeants tried to smother the flames with coats and jackets. By the time an ambulance arrived, 70% of Morrison's body was burned. He was declared dead on arrival at Fort Myers Army Dispensary.

Morrison's self immolation, his wife Anne soon explained, expressed "his concern over the great loss of life and human suffering caused by the war in Viet Nam. He was protesting our government's deep military involvement in this war." The suicide ended a life centered on religion since boyhood. Morrison was born in Erie, PA. When he was 13, his widowed mother moved the family to Chautauqua, N.Y., where he became the first youth in the county to win the Boy Scout God and Country Award. He was raised a Presbyterian, but gradually became interested in Quaker beliefs, particularly pacifism, while a student at Wooster College. He later studied at a Presbyterian seminary in Pittsburgh and at the University of Edinburgh, and joined the Society of Friends in 1959. Since 1962, he had been executive-secretary of the Stony Run Friends Meeting in Baltimore. In recent months, Morrison had been deeply disturbed about U.S. bombing in Viet Nam, although colleagues detected no outside sign of a psychosis that might explain his death.[1]

[1]*Time*, November 12, 1965, 68.

Name _____

Date _____

Poetic Distance

Out, Out—

The buzz saw snarled and rattled in the yard
And made dust and dropped stove-length sticks of wood,
Sweet-scented stuff when the breeze drew across it.
And from there those that lifted eyes could count
Five mountain ranges one behind the other   5
Under the sunset far into Vermont.
And the saw snarled and rattled, snarled and rattled,
As it ran light, or had to bear a load.
And nothing happened: day was all but done.
Call it a day, I wish they might have said   10
To please the boy by giving him the half hour
That a boy counts so much when saved from work.
His sister stood beside them in her apron
To tell them "Supper." At the word, the saw,
As if to prove saws knew what supper meant,   15
Leaped out at the boy's hand, or seemed to leap—
He must have given the hand. However it was,
Neither refused the meeting. But the hand!
The boy's first outcry was a rueful laugh,
As he swung toward them holding up the hand,   20
Half in appeal, but half as if to keep
The life from spilling. Then the boy saw all—
Since he was old enough to know, big boy
Doing a man's work, though a child at heart—
He saw all spoiled. "Don't let him cut my hand off—   25
The doctor, when he comes. Don't let him, sister!"
So. But the hand was gone already.
The doctor put him in the dark of ether.
He lay and puffed his lips out with his breath.
And then—the watcher at his pulse took fright.   30
No one believed. They listened at his heart.
Little—less—nothing!—and that ended it.
No more to build on there. And they, since they
Were not the one dead, turned to their affairs.

—Robert Frost

The Poet as Reporter

Part I: On the Death of Norman Morrison

1. Categorize the factual information which the three poems provide concerning the late Norman Morrison. Use only information which could have been used by a newspaper report.

2. What do the poets "say" that the journalistic account does not reflect? Give at least two examples.

3. What are some of the "best words" in each poem that communicate the information in a different way than the journalistic account? Why are they the "best"?

	"Best Words"	Reason
Ferguson		
Mitchell		
Starbuck		

Part II: On the Death of a Young Boy

1. Reduce Frost's poem "Out, Out—" to a newspaper notice answering who, what, where, how, when, and why. Use only facts provided by the poem.

2. For consideration:

   a. Is your prose account better than the poem? Why? Why not?

   b. What are the "best words" in the poem? Why?

   c. What is achieved by the inclusion of the following details in the poem?
      ll.4–6:

Name _____

Date _____

ll. 10–12:

ll. 33–34:

Lesson 2:

The Modes of Discourse

Objectives

- To introduce students to the concepts of language as the medium of literature and to discourse as the framework within which literature is structured
- To establish poetry within the context of the varied modes of discourse

Notes to the Teacher

Just as the painter works with paint and canvas, the musician with sound, and the dancer with bodily movement, so the raw material of the writer is language. Whether spoken or written or both, literature is only possible when an author gives additional organization to what is already organized within language itself: sounds in varied patterns which share a certain significance (i.e., refer to a reality) within the group which makes use of them. It is then the task of the writer-as-artist to organize language in terms of both purpose and audience. It is this organization that determines whether prose or poetry will provide the "best words" for the occasion. The emphasis on purpose and audience in any use of language implies a communication process: a speaker encodes an idea (puts into words a message) which is heard (or read) by a listener (an audience of one or many). Of course, the speaker and listener must share a common understanding of the medium (language). Breakdown in communication will obviously occur when the listener does not understand the meaning of words or how they are used within a given context. Likewise, a listener will be at a loss if the purpose of "the message" is misinterpreted, as would be the case, for example, in a literal interpretation of a figurative statement.

Students can be prepared to understand the uniqueness of poetic discourse in relation to what we might term the grammatical and rhetorical modes. The characteristics of each mode can be described by making use of the concrete examples provided in the activities of this lesson.

Aristotle implied a theory of modes in his two treatises on rhetoric and poetics. The "language of prose is distinct from that of poetry," he indicated, and no one resorts to the techniques of rhetoric or poetry "in teaching mathematics." Everyday discourse demands the "grammatical mode," the prose of direct communication, the language of immediate survival and straightforward facts.

Procedure

1. Provide students with an understanding of the necessary terms: medium, language, modes of discourse, communication process.

2. Distribute **Handout 4.** Read the three selections with the students, and ask them to point out similarities and differences.

   Suggested Responses:
   Similarities:
   All three deal with the Sacco-Vanzetti trial.
   Differences:
   Passage 1 is clear, logical, factual, and direct, with "words in their best order" in order to present information.
   Passage 2 attempts primarily to persuade and sway its audience by emotional, as well as logical, appeals. Although the arrangement of words reflects the form of a poem, it is what is usually called a "found" poem, an arrangement of words from a prose passage to reflect traditional poetic form. These lines reflect the emotion of the moment, the poetic instinct that a serious occasion often evokes, rather than the carefully crafted piece of writing that we call poetical.
   Passage 3 attempts to make the most of the resources of language in order to create an effort that is artistic and entertaining (in an intellectual sense). It attempts to use "the best words in the best order." The focus is not on the facts but on what the facts mean: justice has been denied.

It does not even mention the specific case of Sacco-Vanzetti which was a cause cèlèbre of the twenties. The incident has cosmic implications: the earth will no longer be fertile, the sun will not shine ("We shall die in darkness, and be buried in the rain."). By means of carefully chosen images which carry the weight of their symbolism well, the poet has imaginatively expressed the theme and mood. Although additional qualifications and clarifications will eventually be necessary, these characteristics will allow students to begin to differentiate modes of discourse according to style and purpose.

3. Based on their observations concerning the three passages on **Handout 4,** students should be prepared to come to some conclusions concerning *Modes of Discourse.* Have them work in small groups to summarize their conclusions by completing **Handout 5,** Part I.

   Suggested Responses: See Table 1.

4. Have students further clarify their understanding of the three modes of discourse by the completion of **Handout 5,** Part II. Students should be prepared to explain their analogies and create at least one original category.

   Suggested Responses: See Table 2.

Table 1

	Grammatical	Rhetorical	Poetical
Purpose	to inform	to persuade	to entertain
Ways in which language is used	clear; direct; factual; ordinary	unusual; for effect; manipulated; attention getting	special; playful; making the most of the resources of language
Literary model	dictionary; science text	political speech; sermon; advertisement	formal poetry; poetic passage in any form of literature

Table 2

	Grammatical	Rhetorical	Poetical
Light	street light	a red light	Christmas tree light
Line	straight line	dividing line on highway	geometric design
Bodily movement	walking	pointing	dancing
Glass	clear	tinted	stained
Sound	talking	preaching	singing

The Modes of Discourse: Examples

Passage 1

"On May 5, 1920, two professed anarchists named Nicola Sacco and Bartolomeo Vanzetti were arrested on charges that they had killed two men in a payroll robbery at South Braintree, Massachusetts. Both men were immigrants, neither could speak English very well and both had avoided the World War I draft on ideological grounds. To some aroused Americans, the evidence against Sacco and Vanzetti seemed inconclusive, and many were convinced that the two men were the victims of raw prejudice because they were foreigners, radicals and draft-dodgers. Nevertheless, after seven years of litigation and uproar, the men were executed."[1]

Passage 2

Last Speech to the Court

I have talk a great deal of myself
but I even forgot to name Sacco.
Sacco too is a worker,
from his boyhood a skilled worker, lover of work,
with a good job and pay,
a bank account, a good and lovely wife,
two beautiful children and a neat little home
at the verge of a wood, near a brook.

Sacco is a heart, a faith, a character, a man;
a man, lover of nature, and mankind;
a man who gave all, who sacrifice all
to the cause of liberty and to his love for mankind:
money, rest, mundane ambition,
his own wife, his children, himself
and his own life.

Sacco has never dreamt to steal, never to assassinate.
He and I have never brought a morsel
of bread to our mouths, from our childhood to today
which has not been gained by the sweat of our brows.
Never . . .

[1]*This Fabulous Century,* Vol. 3 (New York: Time/Life Books, 1969), 26.

Oh, yes, I may be more witful, as some have put it;
I am a better babbler than he is, but many, many times
in hearing his heartful voice ringing a faith sublime,
in considering his supreme sacrifice, remembering his heroism,
I felt small at the presence of his greatness
and found myself compelled to fight back
from my eyes the tears,
and quanch my heart
trobling to my throat to not weep before him:
this man called thief and assassin and doomed.

But Sacco's name will live in the hearts of the people
and in their gratitude when Katzmann's bones
and yours will be dispersed by time;
when your name, his name, your laws, institutions,
and your false god are but a dim rememoring
of a cursed past in which man was wolf
to the man . . .

If it had not been for these thing
I might have live out my life
talking at street corners to scorning men.
I might have die, unmarked, unknown, a failure.
Now we are not a failure.
This is our career and our triumph. Never
in our full life could we hope to do such work
for tolerance, for justice, for man's understanding
of man, as now we do by accident.

Our words, our lives, our pains—nothing!
The taking of our lives—lives of a good shoemaker and a poor
fishpeddler—
all! That last moment belongs to us—
that agony is our triumph.

—Bartolomeo Vanzetti

Passage 3

Justice Denied in Massachusetts

Let us abandon then our gardens and go home
And sit in the sitting-room.
Shall the larkspur blossom or the corn grow under this cloud?
Sour to the fruitful seed
Is the cold earth under this cloud,
Fostering quack and weed, we have marched upon but cannot conquer;
We have bent the blades of our hoes against the stalks of them.

Let us go home, and sit in the sitting-room.
Not in our day
Shall the cloud go over and the sun rise as before,
Beneficent upon us
Out of the glittering bay,
And the warm winds be blown inward from the sea
Moving the blades of corn
With a peaceful sound.
Forlorn, forlorn,
Stands the blue hay-rack by the empty mow.
And the petals drop to the ground,
Leaving the tree unfruited.
The sun that warmed our stooping backs and withered the weed uprooted—
We shall not feel it again.
We shall die in darkness, and be buried in the rain.

What from the splendid dead
We have inherited—
Furrows sweet to the grain, and the weed subdued—
See now the slug and the mildew plunder.
Evil does overwhelm
The larkspur and the corn;
We have seen them go under.

Let us sit here, sit still,
Here in the sitting-room until we die;
At the step of Death on the walk, rise and go;
Leaving to our children's children this beautiful doorway,
And this elm,
And a blighted earth to till
With a broken hoe.

—Edna St. Vincent Millay

17

Name _____

Date _____

The Modes of Discourse

Part I:

Definition/Description: Summarize your conclusions about the modes of discourse.

	Grammatical	Rhetorical	Poetical
Purpose			
Ways in which language is used			
Literary model			

Part II:

Analogies: Refine your understanding by creating analogies for the modes.

	Grammatical	Rhetorical	Poetical
Light			
Line			
Bodily movement			
Glass			
Sound			

Lesson 3:
"The Voice That Is Great Within Us"

Objectives

- To introduce students to the realm of subjective experience which generates poetic response
- To describe the conventions and characteristics of "confessional poetry"
- To emphasize the role of the speaker in poetic discourse

Notes to the Teacher

Poetry, like all forms of creative endeavor, is self-expression. The poem becomes an "objective" reality only to the extent that it is understood in terms of its "subjective" origins. Norman H. Holland discusses the poetic voice in his *Poems in Persons:*

> If we treat "objective and "subjective" as two neat little boxes and insist on sorting aspects of experience into one or the other, we shall have no way of accounting for literary creation or recreation, or all the other kinds of total experience that combine the two . . . The more objective you are, the more removed from pure experience; the more subjective, the more you lose sight of and distort the objective reality. Finally, "objective reality" and "pure experience" are themselves only useful fictions, vanishing points we approach but never reach.[1]

On the subjective-objective continuum, many poets choose a voice that at least suggests a personal or even autobiographical involvement within the world of their poem. Others assume a mask, a persona which distances (objectifies) the content of the poem, both intellectually and emotionally, from themselves. Consequently, it is easier to find evidence of the poet, the speaker, the person, in some poems than in others. As readers, we cannot assume that the poetic voice is necessarily autobiographical. Plato called poets "liars"; in truth, they are fabricators of an imaginary world that does not have to be real nor reflect even the reality that is their own.

In reading and discussing the poems in this lesson, it is important to stress that even though these poems seem to be examples of "true confessions" (and may indeed be just that), it is not biography that we are looking for, but a record of how the real or imagined experiences of these poems give greater insight into the feelings, thoughts, and experiences of everyone who reads them. That is, in part, what makes them poems.

Just as revealing as what poets often say about themselves in their poems is what they say about the poetic process itself: why they write poetry, when it happens, and what happens when it happens. A whole body of poetry exists which explores these issues. Students may gain additional insight into the characteristics of the poetic process by an investigation of some of these revealing statements.

Procedure

1. Distribute **Handout 6,** and have students read Patrick Middleton's "Daddy" and "Happy Father's Day." Ask students to summarize what each poem reveals about its speaker. Point out that these "facts" in themselves are either commonplace or lend themselves to an emotional or overly dramatic treatment. Then ask students to consider whether the poet has controlled the experience so that the poems avoid sentimentality. Answers will vary.

   Suggested Responses:

Autobiographical Facts	Poetic Treatment
"Daddy"	
Father and son (the speaker) are alienated.	*"your pied-piping no longer pipes through. . ."*
Son looks back at unpleasant childhood.	*"a black trap/with no seeing eye . . . a point of view filled with cracks"*

[1]Norman H. Holland, *Poems in Persons* (New York: W.W. Norton & Co., 1975), prologue, 2.

21

At present the speaker wonders how he lost his love for his father.	*was it "that menacing spy . . . who lives in the back of my eye"? (guilt, conscience?)*
"Happy Father's Day" *Father visits son, but is turned away by prison guard.*	*Guard's "smile" is accompanied by the irony of his comment and the situation (Father's Day and 25 years separation).*
Speaker "cries" for his loss and for the guard's children.	*Speaker shows that he can feel and is not "some other guy" (the speaker of "Daddy"); he also "cries" for the children of an "untouchable man," one who cannot feel.*

2. Distribute **Handout 7.** Read Sylvia Plath's "Daddy" to the students, asking them to circle the words and phrases which they feel reflect confessional aspects of the poem. These are some of the words which reflect the speaker's relationship with the father:

    *   "black shoe/In which I have lived like a foot": stepped on and subjugated
    *   "I have had to kill you": wipe you out of memory
    *   "a bag full of God": ambivalent attitude, one of awe and hatred
    *   "I used to pray to recover you": sense of guilt at loss of dead father ("I was ten when they buried you.")

*   "your foot, your root": father was of German origin
*   "may well be a Jew": the speaker describes the father-daughter relationship as though she were a Jew and her father was Hitler
*   "I tried to die": suicide attempts
*   ". . . made a model of you . . . and I said I do, I do": looked for the image of her father in the man she married

3. Point out that although all three poems considered here are autobiographical, it is not always safe to assume that the information in a poem is necessarily about the poet. A poet can always be a fabricator. Likewise, it is the quality of the fabrication, coupled with the intensity of the experience, which usually translates into poetic discourse.

4. Distribute **Handout 8,** Poems About Poetry. As an independent project, students could obtain copies and study one or more of the poems listed, all of which deal with some aspect of the poetic process. After students have completed their research, they could report back to the class, write a reaction to the poem(s), or write their own theories of poetry based on what they have concluded thus far. As a culminating activity, students may categorize the poems in terms of the poetic process (inspiration, organization, use of material, revision, audience response, etc.). Some students may then research a specific category as the basis for further analytical or personal response.

Name _____

Date _____

Poems about Experiences

Consider the experiences related in these two poems.

Daddy

Concerning your letter in which you plead:
society will have no part of me,

with my bitterness,
with my greed,

You're too late, Daddy Dear, your pied-piping
no longer pipes through these pickled ears.

It was such a dark youth, a black trap
with no seeing-eye,

each blink, each thought, a cul-de-sac,
a point-of-view filled with cracks.

And I, with my pick-up sticks and toy jacks,
waited, dumb as stones;

First Confession was twelve hours long:
Bless me, Father, for the wrong, wrong,

wrong I've done: I drove my Daddy away.
Penance. Penance! I did my penance and then some.

Twenty years later you drifted by,
and I saw a cloudy forecast in the sky.

Did you think the son would shine?
I tried . . . I tried . . .

You asked forgiveness, and I thought:
What was there to forgive?

A son's love is no mere camel's
burden of spices.

This, Daddy Dear, is a much more
serious crisis.

Is it comforting to you?
I once carved your name on a pew,

a catholic boy's graffiti,
an S.O.S from the needy.

Who snuffed out that pristine candle?
Was it Time, or I, or that menacing spy

who joined me in the womb
and lives in the back of my eye?

It doesn't matter, the flame went out,
and now I am some other guy.

—Patrick Middleton

Happy Father's Day

Today you drove 160 miles
and they turned you away.
When the captain of the guards
informed me a mistake had been made:
"Sorry, Middleton, you do have one visit
left for the month. Tell your father
he can come back next weekend,"
I locked the tears in my eyes,
for men in prison aren't supposed to cry.
How I wanted to choke his regrets,
to swat his smile like one does a housefly.
But, no.
Instead, I hid in my closet of a cell
and I cried.
I cried because this Father's Day,
our first together in 25 years,
would have to wait another year;
I cried because this Father's Day
I would kiss your cheek
for the first time in 25 years;
I cried because this Father's Day
I would whisper in your ear,
                "I love you, Dad,"
for the first time in 25 years.

And I cried for the sons and daughters
of the "untouchable" man who turned you away.

—Patrick Middleton

24

Name _____

Date _____

For Discussion:
Consider how each poem reveals its speaker. Contrast the grammatical statement of facts with the poetic treatment.

Autobiographical Facts	Poetical Treatment
"Daddy"	
"Happy Father's Day"	

Name _____

Date _____

Daddy

You do not do, you do not do
Any more, black shoe
In which I have lived like a foot
For thirty years, poor and white,
Barely daring to breathe or Achoo.

Daddy, I have had to kill you.
You died before I had time—
Marble-heavy, a bag full of God,
Ghastly statue with one grey toe
Big as a Frisco seal

And a head in the freakish Atlantic
Where it pours bean green over blue
In the waters off beautiful Nauset.
I used to pray to recover you.
Ach, du.

In the German tongue, in the Polish town
Scraped flat by the roller
Of wars, wars, wars.
But the name of the town is common.
My Polack friend

Says there are a dozen or two.
So I never could tell where you
Put your foot, your root,
I never could talk to you.
The tongue stuck in my jaw.

It stuck in a barb wire snare.
Ich, ich, ich, ich,

I could hardly speak.
I thought every German was you.
And the language obscene

An engine, an engine
Chuffing me off like a Jew.
A Jew to Dachau, Auschwitz, Belsen.
I began to talk like a Jew.
I think I may well be a Jew.

The snows of the Tyrol, the clear beer of
   Vienna
Are not very pure or true.
With my gypsy ancestress and my weird
   luck
And my Taroc pack and my Taroc pack
I may be a bit of a Jew.

I have always been scared of *you*,
With your Luftwaffe, your gobbledygoo.
And your neat moustache
And your Aryan eye, bright blue.
Panzer-man, panzer-man, O You—

Not God but a swastika
So black no sky could squeak through.
Every woman adores a Fascist,
The boot in the face, the brute
Brute heart of a brute like you.

You stand at the blackboard, daddy,
In the picture I have of you,
A cleft in your chin instead of your foot
But no less a devil for that, no not
Any less the black man who

Bit my pretty red heart in two.
I was ten when they buried you.
At twenty I tried to die
And get back, back, back to you.
I thought even the bones would do.

But they pulled me out of the sack,
And they stuck me together with glue.
And then I knew what to do.
I made a model of you,
A man in black with a Meinkampf look

And a love of the rack and the screw.
And I said I do, I do.
So daddy, I'm finally through.

Name _____

Date _____

The black telephone's off at the root,
The voices just can't worm through.

If I've killed one man, I've killed two—
The vampire who said he was you
And drank my blood for a year,
Seven years, if you want to know.
Daddy, you can lie back now.

There's a stake in your fat black heart
And the villagers never liked you.
They are dancing and stamping on you.
They always *knew* it was you.
Daddy, daddy, you bastard, I'm through.

—Sylvia Plath

Name _____

Date _____

Poems about Poetry

Ashbery, Hohn, "A Man of Words" (from *Self-Portrait in a Convex Mirror*, Viking Press, 1972)

Ferlinghetti, Lawrence, "Constantly Risking Absurdity" (from *A Coney Island of the Mind*, New Directions, 1958)

Francis, Robert, "Catch" (from *The Orb Weaver*, Wesleyan University Press, 1953)

Francis, Robert, "Pitcher" (from *The Orb Weaver*, Wesleyan University Press, 1953)

Hayden, Robert, "The Performers" (from *Night Blooming Cereus*, October House, 1972)

Hazo, Samuel, "For a Poet Who Writes and Wonders Why" (from *My Sons in God*, University of Pittsburgh Press, 1965)

Hernton, Calvin, "The Distant Drum" (from *New Negro Poets: USA*, Langston Hughes, ed., Indiana University Press, 1964)

MacLeish, Archibald, "Ars Poetica" (from *New and Collected Poems* 1917–1936, Houghton Mifflin Company, 1976)

Moore, Marianne, "Poetry" (from *Collected Poems*, Macmillan Company, 1935)

O'Hara, Frank, "A True Account of Talking to the Sun at Fire Island" (from *Collected Poems*, Alfred A. Knopf, Inc., 1968)

Service, Robert, "Inspiration" (from *The Best of Robert Service*, Dodd, Mead and Company, 1953)

Shakespeare, William, "Not Marble, Nor the Gilded Monuments . . ." (Sonnet 55)

Shapiro, Karl, "As You Say (not without sadness), Poets Don't See, They Feel" (from *Selected Poems*, Random House, 1964)

Snyder, Gary, "As For Poets" (from *The New American Review*, No. 15, 1972)

Strand, Mark, "Eating Poetry" (from *Reasons for Moving*, Athenium Publishers, 1968)

Thomas, Dylan, "In My Craft or Sullen Art" (from *The Poems of Dylan Thomas*, New Directions, 1972)

Wordsworth, William, "The Solitary Reaper"

_____, "I Wandered Lonely as a Cloud"

Lesson 4
The Poem Must Be

Objectives

- To introduce students to an experience of poetry as an objective statement and a work of art
- To describe the characteristics of poetic discourse in terms of formal, linguistic considerations

Notes to the Teacher

After all is said and done (literally), the poem must not only live up to the expectations of the poet, but it must also reflect the great expectations of its audience. It must communicate its meaning in a fresh and original way (the "best words in the best order"). It must, as Archibald MacLeish states in "Ars Poetica," "not mean/But be." It must transcend the mere communication of a message, the manipulation of a metaphor, and the resonance of a rhyme. It must become some *thing* that is all of these things but is only *one* thing as a result.

There are good poems and there are great poems. As a culminating activity, more can be said about this. For now, students will be more at ease if they attempt to understand poetic discourse in terms of what makes it different from other discourse, what makes for "the best words in the best order."

Procedure

1. Distribute **Handout 9.** Have students discuss the definitions of poetry in terms of their present understanding of poetic discourse. Consider:
   a. Which quotations seem to focus the most attention on the role of the poet?
   Answers: Quotations 2 and 6
   b. Which quotations seem to focus on the medium, language?
   Answers: Quotations 1, 4, 5, 7, 8, and 9

c. Which quotations seem to focus on the impact of the poem on its audience?
Answers: Quotations 2, 3, 6, 9, and 10

2. Distribute **Handout 10** and have students discuss "Nobody Comes." Students will likely conclude that the poem is in keeping with the definitions of poetry which emphasize the qualities of the poem itself rather than a focus on the speaker or audience. Even though the speaker is important to an understanding of this poem, what the speaker feels and does not feel and *how* that is communicated are most important.

Suggested Responses:

a. *The poem is characterized by unity of effect: a sense of isolation and detachment. All parts of the poem contribute to this coherence.*
The speaker (1st person), who is only implied in the opening stanza (e.g., the road is "outside" and the telegraph wires lead "to the town"), is eventually revealed in terms of loneliness: "It has nothing to do with me."

b. *The imagery and symbolism are developed in terms of contrast. Isolation is associated with the end of the day when light is "fainting" and "succumbs to the crawl of night." Social involvement is associated with car lights (although an artificial source of light). The telegraph wire, an obvious symbol of communication, "intones to travellers," but is "spectral lyre" for the noncommunicative speaker. The "road," "travellers," and "car" are all "in a world of [their]own." The speaker, "in a blacker air," is "mute" and "alone."*

c. *The poem's impact on its reader, consequently, is that of a shared experience. Indirectly, it describes the feeling of isolation and separation.*

Definitions of Poetry

1. ". . . the art of poetry is simply the art of electrifying language with extraordinary meaning." (Lascelles Abercrombie, *The Theory of Poetry*, New York, 1926, p. 93)

2. ". . . poetry is man's rebellion against being what he is." (James Branch Cabell, *Jurgen*, New York, 1927, p. 333)

3. "If I read a book [and] it makes my whole body so cold no fire can warm me I know *that* is poetry. If I feel physically as if the top of my head were taken off, I know *that* is poetry. These are the only ways I know it. Is there any other way?" (Emily Dickinson, *The Letters of Emily Dickinson*, ed. Thomas H. Johnson, Cambridge, MA., 1958, II, pp. 473–474.)

4. [Poetry] is metaphor, saying one thing and meaning another, the pleasure of ulteriority. Poetry is simply made of metaphor." (Robert Frost, "The Constant Symbol," *Atlantic Monthly*, CLXXVIII, October, 1946, p. 50)

5. "The business of words in prose is primarily to *state*; in poetry, not only to state, but also (and sometimes primarily) to *suggest*." (John Livingston Lowes, *Conventions and Revolt in Poetry*, Boston and New York, 1919, p. 181)

6. "Poetry comes with anger, hunger and dismay; it does not often visit groups of citizens sitting down to be literary together, and would appall them if it did." (Christopher Morley, *John Mistletoe*, Garden City, NY, 1931, p. 55)

7. "Let us understand by poetry all literary production which attains the power of giving pleasure by its form, as distinct from its matter." (Walter Pater, "Winckelmann," *The Renaissance*, London, 1914, p. 230)

8. "Great literature is simply language charged with meaning to the utmost possible degree. . . The language of prose is much less highly charged, that is perhaps the only availing distinction between prose and poesy." (Ezra Pound, *Literary Essays of Ezra Pound*, ed. T. S. Eliot, Norfolk, CT, 1954, pp. 23, 26)

9. "Poetry is a revelation in words by means of the words." (Wallace Stevens, "The Noble Rider and the Sound of Words," *The Necessary Angel*, New York, 1951, p. 33)

10. "Poetry is like shot silk with many glowing colours, and every reader must find his own interpretation according to his ability, and according to his sympathy with the poet." (Alfred, Lord Tennyson, *The Works of Tennyson*, ed. Hallam, Lord Tennyson, New York, 1939, p. 879)

Name _____

Date _____

A Poem for Consideration

Discuss the following poem in terms of the various definitions listed on **Handout 9.**

Nobody Comes

Tree-leaves labour up and down,
    And through them the fainting light
    Succumbs to the crawl of night.
Outside in the road the telegraph wire
    To the town from the darkening land
Intones to travellers like a spectral lyre
    Swept by a spectral hand.

A car comes up, with lamps full-glare,
    That flash upon a tree:
    It has nothing to do with me,
And whangs along in a world of its own,
    Leaving a blacker air;
And mute by the gate I stand again alone,
    And nobody pulls up there.

—Thomas Hardy

Consider the potential impact of the poem in terms of the following:

a. the thoughts and feelings of the speaker

b. the poem itself as a work of art (a manipulation of the medium)

c. the audience appeal

Lesson 5
The Poem Itself: The Structure of Meaning

Objectives

- To review linguistic techniques which enable the poet to communicate meaning
- To examine the contribution of linguistic technique to the development of poetic discourse

Notes to the Teacher

Students all too often confuse art and technique. While it is important that students are able to identify the various ways by which a poet applies craftsmanship to language, the medium, it is just as important that students understand the rationale for technique. A metaphor, for example, must be original, insightful, and appropriate if it is to contribute to the artistry of the poem. Likewise, no technique, no matter how well executed, is justified in itself. It must contribute to the overall artistry of the entire poem.

Procedure

1. Distribute **Handout 11.** (Note: It is assumed that this material is a review for AP students.) Direct students to work in small groups (or individually) in order to create original examples of each of the literary techniques. You may also ask them to cite examples from previous handouts.

2. Engage students in a follow-up discussion during which they consider the following questions:
   a. In what ways do techniques help to communicate literal meaning? Give specific examples. (Used effectively, techniques support meaning in a fresh, insightful way. Examples abound.)
   b. What factors influence the choice of a specific technique in order to communicate meaning? (Meaning, tone, style, subject matter, speaker and other literary factors influence choice of techniques!)

3. Distribute **Handout 12.** Students may work in small groups or individually. Direct them to make marginal notes in which they key (by numbers used on **Handout 11**) all of the techniques which are employed in the poem. Discuss the poem in terms of the various techniques employed.

Suggested Responses:

Imagery: *The imagistic details in the poem are comparable to those on the urn; they are silhouettes, outlines of what is to be perceived. When the poem describes the "leaf-fringed legend" which decorates the urn, details are suggested: a lover in pursuit, a procession of the pious, a deserted village, etc. The level of sensory response demanded of the reader varies in many parts of the poem. A sense of physical movement is often created at different points ("mad pursuit," "struggle to escape," etc.), but the participants are generalized ("men or gods" and "maidens loath"). Likewise, the physical response that is imagined ("a burning forehead, and a parching tongue") is associated not with people directly but with generalized, idealized "happy, happy love."*

Denotation: *Some students will be uncertain of the literal meaning of the following words: unravish'd; sylvan; ecstacy; timbrels; ditties; adieu; cloy'd; lowing; citadel; Attic; brede; Pastoral.*

Connotation: *Most of the epithets have complex and often paradoxical associations ("unravish'd bride," "sylvan historian," "Attic shape," "Fair attitude," "Cold Pastoral"). Also consider random words in their contexts: "happy," "burning forehead," "parching tongue," "green altar."*

Allusion: *Tempe and Arcady are ideal pastoral places, celebrated in ancient Greek literature; the ritual of animal sacrifice to the gods refers to religious prac-*

tice in antiquity; Attica is a name for ancient Athens.

Irony: *Ironic situations pervade most of the poem. In order for the ideal to exist, it must not change, but at the same time all that is ideal must remain unfulfilled, i.e., be imperfect.* ("Bold Lover, never, never canst thou kiss,/Though winning near the goal—").

Understatement: *Various ideas in the poem are understated. For example, the religious ideas of the poem are not emphasized, yet the question is asked: "What men or gods are these." The urn itself is said to "tease us out of thought/As doth eternity." The poem is as much a religious quest as it is an artistic one: "Beauty is truth, truth beauty" is a means of interpreting experience, real or imagined, in the light of eternity.*

Hyperbole: *The speaker describes "human passion" in terms of "ecstasy" and physical extremes ("burning forehead, and a parching tongue") and proceeds to attribute it to the "marble men and maidens" on the urn.*

Paradox: *The urn is an "unravish'd bride." It is the "foster-child of Silence," yet it expresses itself "more sweetly" than the poem itself. "Heard melodies are sweet, but those unheard/Are sweeter."*

Simile: *The only simile is: "Thou, silent form, dost tease us out of thought/As doth eternity."*

Metaphor: *Most of the metaphoric statements are contained within the personifications and apostrophes.*

Personification: *"unravish'd bride"; "foster-child"; "Sylvan historian"; "happy boughs"*

Apostrophe: *The urn is directly addressed throughout the poem, as are details portrayed upon it ("pipes," the "Bold Lover," the "happy boughs").*

Symbol: *Various images of the poem function on the symbolic level. The urn itself becomes a symbol for the permanence of art, and the speaker is the representative of the world of change, reality. The stasis of the art world is represented in symbolic terms: the love pursuit, the religious/social ritual, the unheard melodies of the piper/poet.*

Tone: *The tone is both questioning and philosophically conclusive. It is sensitive to both the perfection which can be captured in the ideal world of art and the basis for it in the real world of experience and change.*

Name _____

Date _____

Literary Techniques: Review

After each defined term, write an original example or one from poems on previous handouts.

1. Imagery: language that appeals to the senses

2. Denotation: dictionary definition of a word

3. Connotation: emotions and ideas associated with a word

4. Allusion: reference to something in history or literature

5. Irony: discrepancy between expectation and reality or between words and intention

6. Understatement: a statement which means less than what is intended

7. Hyperbole: a statement of exaggeration

8. Paradox: an apparent contradiction that conveys truth

9. Simile: direct comparison of two essentially unlike things, using "like" or "as"

10. Metaphor: comparison of two unlike things

11. Personification: attribution of human characteristics to a creature, idea, or object

12. Apostrophe: direct address to an inanimate object or idea

13. Symbol: anything that has a meaning of its own but also stands for something beyond itself

14. Tone: attitude revealed toward the subject

Name _____

Date _____

Literary Techniques: Application

Directions: Read the following poem carefully. Identify various techniques by placing numbers in the margin which correspond to the numbers used on **Handout 11.** Be prepared to discuss the poem in terms of the effectiveness of various techniques employed.

Ode on a Grecian Urn

I

Thou still unravish'd bride of quietness,
    Thou foster-child of Silence and slow Time,
Sylvan historian, who canst thus express
    A flowery tale more sweetly than our rhyme:
What leaf-fringed legend haunts about thy shape
    Of deities or mortals, or of both,
        In Tempe or the dales of Arcady?
    What men or gods are these? what maidens loth?
What mad pursuit? What struggle to escape?
    What pipes and timbrels? What wild ecstasy?   10

II

Heard melodies are sweet, but those unheard
    Are sweeter; therefore, ye soft pipes, play on;
Not to the sensual ear, but, more endear'd,
    Pipe to the spirit ditties of no tone.
Fair youth, beneath the trees, thou canst not leave
    Thy song, nor ever can those trees be bare;
        Bold Lover, never, never canst thou kiss,
Though winning near the goal—yet, do not grieve;
    She cannot fade, though thou has not thy bliss.
        For ever wilt thou love, and she be fair!   20

III

Ah, happy, happy boughs! that cannot shed
    Your leaves, nor ever bid the Spring adieu;
And, happy melodist unwearied,
    For ever piping songs for ever new;
More happy love! more happy, happy love!
    For ever warm and still to be enjoy'd.
        For ever panting, and for ever young;
All breathing human passion far above,
    That leaves a heart high-sorrowful and cloy'd,
        A burning forehead, and a parching tongue.   30

IV

Who are these coming to the sacrifice?
   To what green altar, O mysterious priest,
Lead'st thou that heifer lowing at the skies,
   And all her silken flanks with garlands drest?
What little town by river or sea shore,
   Or mountain-built with peaceful citadel,
     Is emptied of this folk, this pious morn?
     And, little town, thy streets for evermore
   Will silent be; and not a soul to tell
     Why thou art desolate, can e'er return.   40

V

O Attic shape! Fair attitude! with brede
   Of marble men and maidens overwrought,
With forest branches and the trodden weed;
   Thou, silent form, dost tease us out of thought
As doth eternity: Cold Pastoral!
   When old age shall this generation waste,
     Thou shalt remain, in midst of other woe
   Than ours, a friend to man, to whom thou say'st,
'Beauty is truth, truth beauty,'—that is all
   Ye know on earth, and all ye need to know.   50

—John Keats

Lesson 6
The Poem Itself: The Structure of Sound

Objectives

- To review the techniques which enable the poet to structure sound patterns
- To examine the contribution of sound techniques to the development of poetic discourse

Notes to the Teacher

Sound techniques are often easy to identify but difficult to justify. A lot of what happens in a poem's mood and tone is caused by the way the poem sounds. Students should be able to relate to this concept by the way the words of popular songs are enhanced by music.

Procedure

1. Distribute **Handout 13.** Direct students to work in small groups and match the terms and definitions with the literary examples. It is assumed that AP students are already somewhat familiar with this material. Multiple responses are appropriate but should be justified.

   Suggested Responses:

1. *c, i, o, and t*	4. *a, j, l, and m*
2. *a and j or s, l,*	5. *a, f, g, h, i, j,*
m, and n	*and o*
3. *p, q, and r*	6. *l and t*

2. Distribute **Handout 14.** Engage in a follow-up discussion of sound patterns used in the poems on this handout. Use the following two questions to guide the discussion:
   a. In what ways do sound techniques help to structure a poem?
   b. How, in Alexander Pope's words, is "sound" an "echo to the sense" (or meaning) that a poem attempts to communicate? Give specific examples.

   Suggested Responses:
   a. *As Pope himself demonstrates, meter can suggest a mood. In his lines from "An Essay on Criticism," for example, Ajax's physical efforts are echoed in a strained series of spondees ("rock's vast weight," "line, too, labours" and "words move slow"). In similar fashion, he alternately demonstrates the euphonious and cacophonous effects of words selected for their sound quality.*

   b. *Updike's "Player Piano" resounds with sound effects. The alternating lines of trochaic pentameter and tetrameter echo the metallic music of the piano itself. The varied use of alliteration ("stick," "click," "snicker") and assonance ("paper," "caper," "man," "band," "hand," etc.) also contribute to the variety of music which the poem is all about.*

   Hazo's "Preface to a Poetry Reading" does not attempt to demonstrate Pope's dictum but to emphasize the need for the ear to hear the sound of a poem in order to comprehend its total meaning.

   Jonson's "Fit" points to the restrictions which rhyme and other techniques impose upon sense. At the same time, he ironically demonstrates the artful way in which technique can complement the meaning of the words. Jonson's lines are also a "fit," an outburst, but in a very constrained form.

Name _____

Date _____

Sound Techniques: Review

Match the following terms with the quotations. Some quotations may require only one answer; others may require several.

a. iambic   f. monometer   k. hexameter   p. caesura
b. trochaic   g. dimeter   l. alliteration   q. cadence
c. anapestic   h. trimeter   m. assonance   r. free verse
d. dactylic   i. tetrameter   n. onomatopoeia   s. blank verse
e. spondaic   j. pentameter   o. rhyme   t. couplet

_____ 1. "I sprang to the stirrup, and Joris, and he;
          I galloped, Dirck galloped, we galloped all three."   (Browning)

_____ 2. "The buzz-saw snarled and rattled in the yard
          And made dust and dropped stove-length sticks of wood,
          Sweet-scented stuff when the breeze drew across it."   (Frost)

_____ 3. "There was a child went forth every day,
          And the first object he looked upon, that object he became,
          And that object became part of him for the day or a certain part of the day,
          Or for many years or stretching cycle of years."   (Whitman)

_____ 4. "Thou still unravish'd bride of quietness
          Thou foster-child of Silence and slow Time. . ."   (Keats)

_____ 5.

Ode To Ben Jonson

Ah Ben!
Say how or when
Shall we, thy guests,
Meet at those lyric feasts,
    Made at the Sun,
The Dog, the Triple Tun?
Where we such clusters had
As made us nobly wild, not mad;
    And yet each verse of thine
Outdid the meat, outdid the frolic wine.   (Herrick)

_____ 6. "Double, double, toil and trouble
          Fire brew and caldron bubble."   (Shakespeare)

Name _____

Date _____

Sound and Sense in Poems

Sound and Sense

True ease in writing comes from art, not chance,
As those move easiest who have learned to dance.
'Tis not enough no harshness gives offense,
The sound must seem an echo to the sense:
Soft is the strain when Zephyr gently blows,
And the smooth stream in smoother numbers flows;
But when loud surges lash the sounding shore,
The hoarse, rough verse should like the torrent roar;
When Ajax strives some rock's vast weight to throw,
The line too labors, and the words move slow;
Not so, when swift Camilla scours the plain,
Flies o'er the unbending corn, and skims along the main.
Hear how Timotheus' varied lays surprise,
And bid alternate passions fall and rise!

—Alexander Pope
(from "An Essay on Criticism")

Player Piano

My stick fingers click with a snicker
And, chuckling, they knuckle the keys;
Light-footed, my steel feelers flicker
And pluck from these keys melodies.

My paper can caper; abandon
Is broadcast by dint of my din,
And no man or band has a hand in
The tones I turn on from within.

At times I'm a jumble of rumbles,
At others I'm light like the moon,
But never my numb plunker fumbles,
Misstrums me, or tries a new tune.

—John Updike

Preface to a Poetry Reading

Since eyes are deaf and ears are blind to words
in all their ways, I speak the sounds I write,
hoping you see what somehow stays unheard
and hear what never is quite clear to sight.

—Samuel Hazo

from A Fit of Rhyme Against Rhyme

Rhyme, the rack of finest wits,
That expresseth but by fits
    True conceit,
Spoiling senses of their treasure,
Cozening judgment with a measure,
    But false weight;
Wresting words from their true calling,
Propping verse for fear of falling
    To the ground;
Jointing syllables, drowning letters,
Fast'ning vowels as with fetters
    They were bound!
Soon as lazy thou wert known,
All good poetry hence was flown,
    And are banished.

—Ben Jonson

Lesson 7

Poetry in the Marketplace

Objectives

- To investigate the roots of the poetic instinct in popular culture
- To examine the development of poetic sensitivity which is reflected in the development of popular poetry

Notes to the Teacher

There are some who would argue that poetic discourse is a rarefied form of communication accessible only to the intellectual. Others would maintain that poetry has its roots in popular culture and that "folk poetry" and "pop poetry" are the only ways that genuinely felt experience is preserved. The conflict, as ancient as the one between the followers of Apollo and Dionysus, is not likely to be resolved.

However, a taste for Donne and Eliot does not necessarily exclude an acceptance of Whitman and Ferlinghetti. Nor is it necessary to dismiss the efforts of song lyricists such as Paul Simon and Bruce Springsteen. All communication of thoughts and feelings can be encompassed by poetic discourse, and the voice and style vary as much as the shape of the message and the expectations of the audience. Poetry is in the marketplace ready for mass consumption. It is perhaps by means of a popular poetry that a feel for and understanding of other forms of poetic expression can eventually be realized.

Procedure

1. Distribute **Handout 15.** If possible, play a recording of the lyrics. ("I Am a Rock" is on *Sounds of Silence* by Simon and Garfunkel and "The Promised Land" is on *Darkness at the Edge of Town* by Bruce Springsteen.) Examine the lyrics with the students and ask them to point out how each song is a poetic effort.

Suggested Response:

Both lyrics deal with some of the disillusionment and discontent which life has to offer. "I Am a Rock" is the cry of someone who has metaphorically isolated himself (an "island," a "fortress," one "shielded in armour") from involvement because of "feelings that have died." With "books" and "poetry to protect" him, he feels that he can escape the pain that can result from the loss of love. "The Promised Land," on the other hand, reflects a more positive approach. Even though the speaker voices his frustration in a series of violent images ("I just want to explode," "Take a knife and cut this pain from my heart"), he alludes to the "promised land" as a symbol of something better to be achieved in time ("If I could take one moment into my hands").

Likewise, both lyrics handle an emotional outburst in a controlled, artful way. Simon's lyrics are understated in their intensity and unified by images and symbols of isolation. Springsteen's are concrete in their physical details, realistic in their use of colloquial diction, and complex in their symbolism.

2. Distribute **Handout 16.** Ask students to "go shopping" in their own cultural marketplace for their choice examples of fresh pop-poetry. After students have examined and collected various samples of poetry from "the marketplace," discuss the following issues:
   a. What accounts for the mass-appeal of the various samples collected?
   b. How are these samples similar to and different from the other samples of poetry which you have encountered?
   c. What accounts for the difference between popular poetry and academic poetry?

Possible Responses:

Most popular poetry is accessible to the great majority of people. It employs familiar diction, is direct in its approach to its subject, and is not very esoteric in its use of figures and symbols. In contrast, much academic poetry challenges the mind and imagination of readers with subtle style and complex development of ideas. Popular poetry tends to be emotional and/or didactic, while academic poetry is more rational and controlled. Popular poetry often does not survive its delivery and context; academic poetry attempts to offer its multiple meanings for ages to come.

Of course this dichotomy is unreal. In fact, many popular poems and poets (e.g., Shakespeare) become a significant part of a sustained, academic tradition. Likewise, many schools of poetry no longer have much of a following, even in academic circles (e.g., Shelley and Longfellow), even though they enjoyed tremendous popularity during their own times.

Pop Poetry

I Am a Rock

A winter's day
In a deep and dark December:
I am alone,
Gazing from my window
To the streets below
On a freshly fallen
   silent shroud of snow.
I am a rock
I am an Island.

I've built walls,
A fortress deep and mighty,
That none may penetrate.
I have no need of friendship;
Friendship causes pain.
It's laughter and it's
   loving I disdain.
I am a rock
I am an island.

Don't talk of love;
I've heard the word before;
It's sleeping in my memory
And I won't disturb the slumber
Of feelings that have died.
If I never loved
I never would have cried.
I am a rock,
I am an island.

I have my books
And my poetry to protect me;
I am shielded in my armour,
Hiding in my room,
Safe within my womb.
I touch no one
   and no one touches me.
I am a rock,
I am an island.

And a rock feels no pain;
And an island never cries.

—Paul Simon
(from *Sounds of Silence*)

The Promised Land

On a rattlesnake speedway in the Utah
   desert
I pick up my money and head back into
   town
Driving cross the Waynesboro county line
I got the radio on and I'm just killing time
Working all day in my daddy's garage
Driving all night, chasing some mirage
Pretty soon little girl I'm gonna take charge.

(Chorus)
The dogs on main street howl,
'Cause they understand,
If I could take one moment into my hands
Mister, I ain't a boy, no, I'm a man,
And I believe in a promised land.

I've done my best to live the right way
I get up every morning and go to work each
   day
But your eyes go blind and your blood runs
   cold
Sometimes I feel so weak I just want to
   explode
Explode and tear this town apart
Take a knife and cut this pain from my heart
Find somebody itching for something to
   start
(Chorus)

There's a dark cloud rising from the desert
   floor
I packed my bags and I'm heading straight
   into the storm
Gonna be a twister to blow everything
   down

That ain't got the faith to stand its ground
Blow away the dreams that tear you apart
Blow away the dreams that break your heart
Blow away the lies that leave you nothing
   but lost and brokenhearted
(Chorus)

I believe in a promised land . . .

—Bruce Springsteen
(from *Darkness on the Edge of Town*)

Name _____

Date _____

Shopping for Poetic Produce

Directions: From your own "marketplace" gather fragments and phrases from song lyrics, advertising, and other sources which you feel reflect a poetic effort on the part of their writers. Be prepared to present them to the class and to explain your choices.

Lesson 8
The World of the Poem—Guidelines for Analysis

Objectives

- To enable students to integrate their understanding of a poem into an analysis and evaluation of its total structure
- To establish a rubric for the evaluation of analytical essays by students

Notes to the Teacher

The initial experience of an amateur literary critic is one of confusion. Every poem is a puzzle to be solved; until the parts are put together, the total picture is not too apparent. If the parts can be understood in isolation, then it is easier to see how they fit together. Students can gain a certain amount of critical confidence initially if they can demonstrate their mastery of at least the technical aspects of a poem. AP students, however, should be capable of going beyond mere technical analysis. They should be prepared to evaluate a poem in terms of fitness: its qualitative, aesthetic use of the resources of its medium.

An analysis of the total structure of a poem is possible only after the parts are understood in relation to the whole. A metaphor by itself may be imaginative, but it is only truly meaningful when it is understood in relation to the total development and organization of the poem.

The ability to evaluate the appropriateness or fitness of various technical aspects of a poem comes with practice. Reading one poem will prepare the way for a more intense reading of the next one. It is important at the outset to employ a methodical approach. Intuitive, impressionistic responses to a literary work may reflect taste, but they do not necessarily reflect understanding. After the initial emotional response is experienced—like or dislike—it must be examined. If dislike is based on a lack of understanding, then the process of analysis can at least qualify a reader to arrive at a more rational rejection.

This lesson provides a systematic means of evaluating the technical aspects of a poem, the issues relevant to the understanding of a poem's total structure, and a rubric for the evaluation of a student's analysis.

Procedure

1. Distribute **Handout 17.** Review the guidelines in conjunction with a class discussion of a poem from a previous handout. Frost's "Out, Out. . .," Plath's "Daddy," Millay's "Justice Denied in Massachusetts," or Keats' "Ode on a Grecian Urn" will serve the purpose. Responses will vary according to the poem under consideration. Use the discussion to clarify any theoretical and technical aspects of literary theory that have been taken for granted up to this point.

2. Discuss with students the organization and development of an analytical essay which they are to complete within a six-to-ten-day period. Include the following points:
   a. Select a poem for analysis from **Handout 18.**
   b. Read the poem in conjunction with the Guidelines for Reading a Poem, **Handout 17.**
   c. Compose a thesis or central idea which you plan to develop in response to the poem.
   d. Plan the ways in which your thesis can be developed by composing tentative topic sentences for the paragraphs. Indicate in your plan how the text of the poem can support each topic sentence.
   e. Organize, develop, and revise your essay according to the Evaluation Rubric provided (**Handout 19**).

Remind students that biographical, historical, and critical material should be used only if it is relevant to the thesis. Likewise, they should analyze technical aspects of the poem only when they relate to the thesis. Students should assume that their readers are familiar with the poem and not waste time paraphrasing it.

Students should be informed if they will be expected to teach their poems to the rest of the class at a later date or share their analytical essays with other members of the class.

Ask students to include a photocopy or typed copy of the poem with their essays.

Name _____

Date _____

Guidelines for Reading a Poem

The following directives and questions are designed to help you read a poem attentively and intensely. They do not add up to an automatic formula which will guarantee your total appreciation and understanding of any one poem. They are intended to help stimulate and organize your thinking about the poem so that you will be prepared to discuss and write about it in detail. Not all of the guidelines are relevant to every poem; your ability to detect this will further develop your critical skills.

Stage One: The Grammatical Level

1. Read the poem once, preferably aloud. This first reading should provide a general impression of what the poem is about and how its ideas are stuctured. What problems does it pose for interpretation?

2. What is the literal message? What aspects of its message (vocabulary and context) are unclear? Use a dictionary and look up the meaning of any unfamiliar words. Do their meanings fit the context?

3. Take note of the sense-appeal which the poem incorporates (imagery). Does one sense dominate?

4. Observe the diction of the poem. Is it awkward, stilted, trite, and vague? Or is it natural, original, energetic, and appropriate?

5. Does the syntax aid in communicating the "message" of the poem effectively? Is the syntax strained and forced or balanced and varied?

6. Read the poem again in order to determine any parts of it that are unclear on the literal level.

Stage Two: The Rhetorical Level

1. Examine the rhetorical situation in the poem, its dramatic structure.
   a. What does it reveal about the speaker and the person spoken to (the addressee)?
   b. What are the purpose and the occasion for the address (or speech)?

2. Be attentive to the emotional appeal, the power of suggestion, of certain words (connotations).

3. What manipulation of meaning (use of rhetorical devices) does the poem engage in to attract attention to itself: figures of speech, antithesis, ironies, parallels, paradoxes, etc.?

4. What manipulations of the readers' emotions or reason does the poem include? Does the poem build on genuine sentiment and sincerity or is it sentimental, forced, and melodramatic? What is the mood which it conveys? Is it logical and insightful, or fallacious and didactic? What is its tone? What is its theme?

5. What manipulations of sound patterns does the poem use: rhyme, rhythm, assonance, alliteration, etc.?

Stage Three: The Poetic Level

1. Do all of the individual parts contribute to the total experience of the poem?

_____ title	_____ sounds	_____ tone
_____ images	_____ diction	_____ external form
_____ figures	_____ allusions	_____ internal form
_____ symbols	_____ syntax	

2. Is the total experience of the poem significant, intense, and greater than its analysis and paraphrase?

Poems for Analysis

"The Good Morrow" (John Donne)

"On My First Son" (Ben Jonson)

"The Collar" (George Herbert)

"Bermudas" (Andrew Marvell)

"The Solitary Reaper" (William Wordsworth)

"Ulysses" (Alfred, Lord Tennyson)

"My Last Duchess" (Robert Browning)

"The Darkling Thrush" (Thomas Hardy)

"Thanatopsis" (William Cullen Bryant)

"The Jewish Cemetery at Newport" (Henry Wadsworth Longfellow)

"More Light, More Light!" (Anthony Hecht)

"The Rose Family" (Robert Frost)

"Anthem for Doomed Youth" (Wilfred Owen)

"Among School Children" (William Butler Yeats)

"Huswifery" (Edward Taylor)

"A Description of the Morning" (Jonathan Swift)

"Love Calls Us to the Things of This World" (Richard Wilbur)

"Lady Lazarus" (Sylvia Plath)

"Pike" (Ted Hughes)

"A Camp in the Prussian Forest" (Randell Jarrell)

"Scottsboro, Too, Is Worth Its Song" (Countee Cullen)

"The Funeral Rites of the Rose" (Robert Herrick)

"To Autumn" (John Keats)

"The Hollow Men" (T.S. Eliot)

"I Think Continually of Those Who Were Truly Great" (Stephen Spender)

"Dover Beach" (Matthew Arnold)

"Ode to the West Wind" (Percy Bysshe Shelley)

"To Althea, from Prison" (Richard Lovelace)

"Is My Team Plowing?" (A.E. Housman)

"To My Mother" (George Barker)

"Florida" (Elizabeth Bishop)

"I, Too, Sing America" (Langston Hughes)

"somewhere I have never travelled, gladly beyond" (E.E. Cummings)

Name _____

Date _____

"Ars Poetica" (Archibald MacLeish)

"Portrait d'une Femme" (Ezra Pound)

"Pied Beauty" (Gerard Manley Hopkins)

"The Soldier" (Rupert Brooke)

A Rubric for Evaluation

Organization and Development

Introduction

____ The thesis is interpretative, based on but transcending the "facts" of the poem.

____ The thesis is organic to the poem and not imposed upon it.

____ The thesis is limited in scope and well supported by the text of the poem itself, with quotations where appropriate.

Body

____ Each paragraph contains a well-developed topic which is directly related to the thesis.

____ Each paragraph contains quotations from the text of the poem. These quotations support the topic.

____ Each paragraph contains transitional elements which emphasize the progression of the ideas.

Content

____ The paper takes into account the literal as well as the symbolic meaning of the poem.

____ The paper analyzes the imagery, diction, and syntax of the poem.

____ The paper examines the dramatic structure of the poem, taking into account the relationship between the speaker and the addressee as well as the function of the poem as "speech."

____ The paper takes into account rhetorical devices which the poem employs as a means of effecting communication.

____ The paper reveals the tone and theme of the poem and analyzes the means by which they are revealed.

____ The paper analyzes the ways in which sound patterns are structured for effects related to the structure of meaning.

____ The paper takes into account how various patterns of meaning and sound give the poem aesthetic unity.

Conclusion

____ It contains no new information or interpretation.

____ A summary provides a well-supported thesis.

Editorial Aspects

____ Word choices reflect precision and maturity.

____ Sentence structure is correct and varied.

____ The entire paper is well edited in terms of capitalization, spelling, and other mechanical details.

Lesson 9
Only the Shadow Knows/Efforts at Evaluation

Objective

• To evaluate students' understanding and application of poetic theory

Notes to the Teacher

At this point, students should feel comfortable with a theory of poetry which emerges from an understanding of the various modes of discourse and the total communication process, as well as aesthetic principles relevant to literary composition: repetition, variation, originality, and fitness. They have had the opportunity to apply their understanding in a variety of ways and should now be ready for a summary evaluation. Many of these considerations will be reinforced in later lessons. A student's performance at this point may not reflect complete mastery. The results of this evaluation serve as an inventory of issues needing more in-depth consideration in the future.

Procedure

1. Distribute **Handouts 20** and **21.** Students should have **Handout 17** (Guidelines for Reading a Poem) from Lesson 8 for reference.

2. Direct students to read the poem on **Handout 20** carefully, and then use **Handout 17** as a guide for recording their responses on **Handout 21.**

   Suggested Responses (Handout 21):
   Grammatical Level:
   1. *General idea: The philosophical conclusions of this "lecture" are inductively arrived at in the two couplets:*
      a. *Love is perfected when it is apparent to all and conceals nothing. (11. 11–12)*
      b. *Love is destroyed by deception. (11. 25–26).*

2. *The vocabulary is quite simple, containing no words unfamiliar to students.*
3. *The diction is somewhat formal, although a first person speaker is employed. The inverted word order and the use of the archaic "thee" suggest poetic diction to students.*
4. *The images are general: the sun, shadows, two lovers walking. There is a lack of sensual detail.*
5. *Students who are very literal minded may be somewhat confused by some of the elements of the poem which make sense in metaphoric and symbolic terms. They will ask: What does the shadow mean? What does the sun stand for? What is "love's day"?*

Rhetorical Level:

1 and 2. Speaker/addressee: The poem is a dramatic monologue. The speaker is personal, although impatient, with his very dramatic opening imperative: "Stand still . . ." (later ironic). He is also somewhat intimate, addressing his "love" again and again in a repetition of personal pronouns. The beloved, however, is somewhat distanced by the "lecture" format. Since "love's day is short," the speaker has assumed that there is little time for debate.

3. *As suggested, the speaker is perhaps interested in persuading his audience more than his addressee that time is short and that love's death will be brought about by shadows/deceptions.*
4. *The following words have predictable connotative impact on students. These responses are also probably in keeping with the poet's rhetorical purpose:*

lecture/philosophy: academic and intellectual associations

shadows: ghostly presence, other worldly; evil; suggestive of darkness and death; mysterious; foreboding of darkness and death

infant loves: infatuation that can develop into a mature, adult love

sun: source of energy; life and growth; wisdom

westwardly: where the sun sets; darkness; the end of the day

decay: mortality; the death of things physical

5. Rhetorical techniques:

The controlling technique is the lecture format with its inductive approach and conclusions stated in two isolated heroic couplets.

Dominant metaphors are the comparison of life to a day and to a journey; love and truth to the sun; non-love, deception, and death to shadows and night.

The poem also incorporates degrees of linguistic and intellectual balance and proportion.

Each stanza begins with an essential idea (stated in couplet form) which is then elaborated upon in the remainder of the stanza. The balance of light/love/truth and shadow/non-love/deception controls the philosophical development of the poem.

6 and 7. Both the tone and the mood are serious and philosophical.

8. The dominant meter is iambic. The rhyme scheme is: a,a,b,b,c,d,d, c,e,e,e. The sound quality of the poem is very restrained and compressed, an echo of the lean philosophical development.

The Poetic Level:

1. The parts: The poem is imaginative and original in its use of the sun-shadow conceit. The sun as a symbol of truth also represents love ("Love is a growing, or full constant light").

The shadow's primary metaphoric function is falseness, but by implication it symbolizes a lack of love and ultimately death itself.

2. The whole: All of the parts of the poem reflect an artful balance and integrity. The grammatical and rhetorical elements are effective in communicating the meaning of the poem, but the amplification of the poetic insight, contained within a very compressed style, transcends any factual or persuasive purpose. Likewise, the sound quality of the lines serves the rationality and control of the poem.

3. General idea/implied theme: The theme of the poem as literally stated (see Grammatical Level, #1) is expanded upon by the rhetorical development within the poem. "Love's philosophy" is much more complex than a basic premise. The poem develops the idea of love as an absolute value in life. No compromise is possible. Deception (the shadow) results in the death of love and a paradoxical death-in-life.

Name _____

Date _____

Critical Reading

Directions: Read the following poem carefully. Then Review **Handout 17,** Guidelines for Reading a Poem. Reread the poem, and use **Handout 21** to take notes and express conclusions. **Handout 21,** when completed, should reflect your present understanding of this poem and poetry in general.

A Lecture upon the Shadow

Stand still, and I will read to thee
A lecture, love, in Love's philosophy.
    These three hours that we have spent,
    Walking here, two shadows went
Along with us, which we ourselves produced;   5
But, now the sun is just above our head,
    We do those shadows tread,
    And to brave clearness all things are reduced.
  So whilst our infant loves did grow,
  Disguises did, and shadows, flow,   10
  From us, and our cares; but, now 'tis not so.

That love hath not attained the highest degree
Which is still diligent lest others see.

Except our loves at this noon stay,
We shall new shadows make the other way.   15
    As the first were made to blind
    Others, these which come behind
Will work upon ourselves and blind our eyes,
If our loves faint and westwardly decline,
    To me thou, falsely, thine,   20
    And I to thee mine actions shall disguise.
The morning shadows wear away,
    But these grow longer all the day,
    But oh, love's day is short, if love decay.

  Love is a growing, or full constant light;   25
  And his first minute after noon is night.

—John Donne

Poetry Analysis Worksheet

This worksheet can be used in conjunction with any poem. When necessary, refer to the directives provided on **Handout 17**, Guidelines for Reading a Poem.

Title _____

Author _____

The Grammatical Level

1. General idea (stated):

2. Vocabulary:

3. Diction:

4. Sense appeal (imagery):

5. Unanswered questions:

The Rhetorical Level

1. The speaker:

2. The addressee:

3. General rhetorical or persuasive purpose:

4. Connotative language:

5. Rhetorical techniques:

6. Tone:

7. Mood:

8. Sound patterns:

The Poetic Level

1. The parts:

2. The whole:

3. General idea/implied theme:

Part II
The Naming of Parts

Introduction

Serious readers need an understanding and appreciation of the complex creative process which produces poetry. The poem itself provides such insight. Moving from the complexity of the poem—an amalgamation of a series of right decisions—the reader eventually realizes that art does not happen accidentally and that the success of the poem is dependent upon multiple choices which consciously or unconsciously occur during its composition. Likewise, readers of poems soon realize that what they bring to the reading—their life experiences, ethnic background, culture, education, linguistic facility—shapes their understanding, interpretation, and appreciation. To educate readers is to realize that

> "The poem" comes into being in the live circuit set up between the reader and "the text." As with the elements of an electric circuit, each component of the reading process functions by virtue of the presence of the others. A specific reader and a specific text at a specific time and place: change any of these, and there occurs a different circuit, a different event—a different poem. The reader focuses his attention on the symbols and on what they help to crystallize out into awareness. Not the words, as uttered sounds or inked marks on a page, constitute the poem, but the structured responses to them. For the reader, the poem is lived-through during his intercourse with the text.[1]

In the following series of lessons, a focus on various "parts" of a poem strengthens the interactive alliance between the reader and the text. Poetry happens when words reveal themselves to readers in ways which are new and noteworthy. When any of the various ways in which words draw attention to themselves (connotation, allusion, etymology, diction, imagery) is foregrounded, poetry begins to occur. When words say more than is literally allowed for (by way of figures, symbols, ambiguity, paradox, irony, understatement, and hyperbole), poetry is in process.

[1]Louise M. Rosenblatt, *The Reader, the Text, the Poem* (Southern Illinois University Press, 1978).

Lesson 10
Words, Words, Words

Objectives

- To emphasize the value of individual word choices in communicating poetic meaning
- To differentiate between the effects of denotative and connotative word choices

Notes to the Teacher

Poetry has its grass-roots origins in the use of individual words. Although it is usually a configuration of words—a striking comparison, for example—which is most memorable, it is sometimes a single word which reverberates and etches itself in memory. Anyone who has read Homer will recall epithets such as "rosy-fingered dawn." E. E. Cummings has made spring "mud-luscious" and "puddle-wonderful" ("Chansons Innocentes"). When students begin to be sensitive to the power of words, they begin to be sensitive to the power of poetry. A feel for words elevates them above the limitations of grammatical discourse.

Procedure

1. Distribute **Handout 22.** Ask students to complete Part I. Ask them to explain their choices. Answers will vary as much as students' varied experiences. Most will agree that it is easier to describe their experience of/or feelings associated with a word than to define (i.e., limit) it. It is easier to define a thing (textbook, bread, carnival) than a quality (love) or something personal (my sister). Students will discover that certain words reflect different tastes (i.e., the Boss, Bruce Springsteen, or The Beatles); different memories or associations (a carnival, my locker, the Big Apple); different contexts (bread, "the staff of life," and "bread," a slang word for "money"). This activity should help sensitize students to the power of words.

2. Give students five minutes to complete Part II. Ask them to share some of their responses. After several have done so, ask them to differentiate between the two categories (circled and uncircled words). At some point, introduce the terms "denotation" (dictionary definition/uncircled words) and "connotation" (emotional, personal associations conveyed by a word/circled words). Most students will already be familiar with the terminology. Discuss denotation in the context of grammatical discourse and connotation in terms of rhetorical discourse.

3. Have students complete Part III of the handout. Hopefully they will choose words which have connotations appropriate to the tone of the poem, one of just anger and violent desperation. Students should find many of the alternatives inappropriate to the poem, especially in reference to the last six lines. Discuss their choices. These are Claude McKay's eight lines:

> If we must die, let it not be like hogs
> Hunted and penned in an inglorious
>   spot,
> While round us bark the mad and
>   hungry dogs,
> Making their mock at our accursed lot.
> If we must die, O let us nobly die,
> So that our precious blood may not be
>   shed
> In vain; then even the monsters we defy
> Shall be constrained to honor us
>   though dead!

Students will undoubtedly want to discuss the violent attitudes which the poem reflects, but they should note that this is modified by the conditional "if," which functions as a framework for its logic. You may wish to point out that Claude McKay, a black writer of the literary movement in the twenties known as the Harlem Renais-

67

sance, was not a direct victim of the social conditions which the poem probably alludes to (i.e., lynchings, especially by the Ku Klux Klan in the south), but was voicing his indignation and anger about the denial of basic human rights to black people everywhere in America. The poem also has a universal message addressed to oppressed people everywhere at any time.

Words, Words, Words

Part I: Circle any of the following words which you feel would be difficult to define. Be prepared to explain your choices.

a textbook   The Boss
a prom   red
my brother or sister   beautiful
love   a carnival
bread   The Big Apple
The Beatles   bugs
my locker   a job

Part II: From the above list, define one of the words which you did not circle and one of the
words which you did circle.

circled word: _____

definition: _____

uncircled word: _____

definition: _____

Part III: Insert one word from the numbered groups which follow to correspond to the
numbered blanks in the first eight lines of the following poem. Choose the word in
each case which you think best expresses what the entire poem is attempting to
communicate, especially in view of the final six lines of Claude McKay's poem.

If we must (1)_____, let it not be like (2)_____
(3)_____ and (4)_____ in a(n) (5)_____ (6)_____,
While round us (7)_____ the (8)_____ and (9)_____ (10)_____,
Making their (11)_____ at our accursed lot.
If we must (1)_____ , let us (12)_____ (1)_____ ,
So that our (13)_____ O (14)_____ may not be (15)_____
In vain; then even the (16)_____ we (17)_____
Shall be (18)_____ to (19)_____ us though dead!
Oh, Kinsmen! We must meet the common foe;
Though far outnumbered, let us show us brave,
And for their thousand blows deal one deathblow!
What though before us lies the open grave?
Like men we'll face the murderous, cowardly pack,
Pressed to the wall, dying, but fighting back!

—Claude McKay

1. pass away/give up/die
2. hogs/dropouts/insects
3. sought/hunted/tracked down
4. penned/trapped/confined
5. strange/inglorious/ordinary
6. location/place/spot
7. bark/growl/yelp
8. mad/upset/angry
9. malnourished/starving/hungry
10. hounds/dogs/pack
11. noise/music/mock
12. nobly/courageously/bravely
13. valuable/precious/pure
14. blood/lives/ideals
15. lost/sacrificed/shed
16. monsters/brutes/villains
17. defy/challenge/confront
18. forced/compelled/constrained
19. respect/honor/remember

Lesson 11

In the Land of Allusion

Objective

- To demonstrate how allusion enriches a poem's structure of meaning

Notes to the Teacher

Allusion provides a substructure of significance on which the poem can build. The poet interfaces the meaning of a poem with the potential rational or emotional evocation of another literary work, an historical event, or a cultural phenomenon.

Anthologies have eased the effort required to research many allusions. However, students should be encouraged occasionally to go beyond what is often a superficial footnote and explore the complete depth of the original source. Likewise, they should attempt to derive a sense of what is referred to by means of contextual clues. Some poets are more inclined to build poems in "the land of allusion" than others. Milton's "On the Late Massacre at Piedmont" and Byron's "The Destruction of Sennacherib" are entirely related to historical and biblical events. Students will no doubt eventually conclude that most poets write for an audience that is educated to both life and literature and that they depend heavily on the reader's background to realize the total impact of the poem.

Procedure

1. Ask students to define "allusion" and to cite some examples which come to mind. Distribute **Handout 23,** and ask students to work together in small groups in order to review the use of allusions in previous handouts. Students should have access to their folders of materials while completing this work.

Suggested Responses:
Handout 1: *The three poems about Norman Morrison allude to the news report,*
the Vietnam War, the anti-war protests, and General Robert McNamara.
Purpose: to underscore the historic despair of those who tried to bring to a close what they viewed as a meaningless war.
Handout 2: *The title of Frost's poem, "Out, Out—," is an allusion to lines from Shakespeare's Macbeth.*

> Out, out, brief candle!
> Life's but a walking shadow.

Purpose: to emphasize Macbeth's realization concerning the meaning of life and death as it parallels the theme in Frost's poem
Handout 4: *Both selections allude to the historic Sacco-Vanzetti trial.*
Handouts 6 and 7: *All of the selections may allude to autobiographical details, but we cannot rule out the possibility that they reflect fictionalized experiences or distorted or edited versions of facts.*
Handout 12: *The ode in general assumes that the reader has some understanding of what a decorative urn, used by the Greeks for storage purposes, looks like.*
Handout 14: *The selection by Pope alludes to various characters in Greek myth. Zephyrus is the god of the west wind. Ajax is the Latin for Aias, who was second only to Achilles in strength and bravery in the Trojan War. From Latin myth, Camilla was a brave warrior maiden in The Aeneid. Timotheus is an ancient poet.*
Handout 15: *Paul Simon's "I Am a Rock" possibly contains an ironic allusion to John Donne's sermon in which he states that "No man is an island." Bruce Springsteen's "The Promised Land" alludes to the biblical "promised land" where the wandering Israelites expected to find "a land flowing with milk and honey" after their forty years in the desert. The speaker implies that only "faith" will allow him and his dreams to survive.*

Handout 21: *Claude McKay's sonnet probably alludes to the activities of the KKK, but there is no textual support for this. Likewise, there is nothing within the text to indicate that the poem deals with a racial issue. The reader's knowledge of history and of the author's background relates these circumstances to a reading and interpretation of the text.*

2. Distribute **Handout 24.** Students, although not necessarily familiar with the historical or biblical allusions, should still have some access to the poems. The context provides essential information. Supply missing information and ask students how it affects their responses. It should provide a greater understanding and appreciation of the poet's purposes in employing allusion.

Background Information:
"On the Late Massacre in Piedmont": On April 24, 1653, the Duke of Savoy ordered the slaughter of over seventeen hundred Waldensians, a Protestant sect living in isolation in the Italian Alps. As Latin Secretary to Cromwell, Milton wrote an official protest. In this sonnet he voices his personal, poetic protest against "the bloody Piedmontese," the "Triple Tyrant" (the Pope's triple crown), and the "Babylonian woe" (a Puritan term for the Roman Catholic church). "When all our fathers worshipped stocks and stones" alludes to the fact that England was still a pagan country when the Waldensians first grouped together into a sect. The reference to sowing the "martyred blood and ashes" from which new life will grow parallels a similar incident in Greek myth.

"The Destruction of Sennacherib": According to the Bible (Kings IV, 19:35), the army of King Sennacherib of Assyria was destroyed in their camp overnight by an "angel of the Lord." This occurred the night before a planned attack on Jerusalem. Ashur was another name for Assyria, and Baal was a divinity. These events historically occurred in the eighth century B.C., and a plague is usually the attributed cause of the destruction of Sennacherib's forces.

Name _____

Date _____

The Land of Allusion

Directions: Give examples of the use of allusion in the following poems, indicating how allusion adds a new level of meaning to the way the poems are developed.

Handout 1:

"Norman Morrison" (Mitchell)

"Norman Morrison" (Ferguson)

"Of Late" (Starbuck)

Handout 2:

"Out, Out—" (Frost)

Handout 4:

"Last Speech to the Court" (Vanzetti)

"Justice Denied in Massachusetts" (Millay)

Handout 6:

"Daddy" (Middleton)

Name _____

Date _____

"Happy Father's Day" (Middleton)

Handout 7:

"Daddy" (Plath)

Handout 12:

"Ode on a Grecian Urn" (Keats)

Handout 14:

"Sound and Sense" (Pope)

Handout 14:

"I Am a Rock" (Simon)

"The Promised Land" (Springsteen)

Handout 21:

"If We Must Die" (McKay)

Saints and Assyrians

Examine the following two poems. Determine to what extent allusion affects your ability to interpret each poem. Record your responses with marginal notes, indicating any parts of the poems with which you experience difficulty. Be prepared to present your conclusions for the questions following each poem, based entirely on evidence within the poem.

On the Late Massacre in Piedmont

Avenge, O Lord, Thy slaughtered saints, whose bones
Lie scattered on the Alpine mountains cold;
Even them who kept Thy truth so pure of old,
When all our fathers worshiped stocks and stones,
Forget not: in Thy book record their groans
Who were Thy sheep, and in their ancient fold
Slain by the bloody Piedmontese, that rolled
Mother with infant down the rocks. Their moans
The vales redoubled to the hills, and they
To heaven. Their martyred blood and ashes sow
O'er all the Italian fields, where still doth sway
The triple Tyrant that from these may grow
A hundredfold, who, having learnt Thy way,
Early may fly the Babylonian woe.

—John Milton

1. Who was killed?

2. By whom?

3. Why?

4. How?

5. Where?

6. What is left unexplained?

The Destruction of Sennacherib

The Assyrian came down like the wolf on the fold,
And his cohorts were gleaming in purple and gold;
And the sheen of their spears was like stars on the sea,
When the blue wave rolls nightly on deep Galilee.

Like the leaves of the forest when summer is green,
That host with their banners at sunset were seen:
Like the leaves of the forest when autumn hath blown,
That host on the morrow lay withered and strown.

For the Angel of Death spread his wings on the blast,
And breathed in the face of the foe as he passed;
And the eyes of the sleepers waxed deadly and chill,
And their hearts but once heaved—and for ever grew still!

And there lay the steed with his nostril all wide,
But through it there rolled not the breath of his pride;
And the foam of his gasping lay white on the turf,
And cold as the spray of the rock-beating surf.

And there lay the rider distorted and pale,
With the dew on his brow, and the rust on his mail:
And the tents were all silent, the banners alone,
The lances unlifted, the trumpet unblown.

And the widows of Ashur are loud in their wail,
And the idols are broke in the temple of Baal;
And the might of the Gentile, unsmote by the sword,
Hath melted like snow in the glance of the Lord!

—George Gordon, Lord Byron

1. Who was killed?

2. By whom?

3. Why?

4. How?

5. Where?

6. What is left unexplained?

Lesson 12

"Mild and Gracious Words": Dealing with Diction

Objectives

- To examine the quality of word choice which is characteristic of poetic discourse
- To contrast different levels of reader expectation in the experience of various poetic styles
- To examine the implications and consequences of a "poetic diction"

Notes to the Teacher

Poets depend on the weight of words to produce an impact upon their readers. Consequently, they choose their words well. Certain periods of literary history expected a more formal discourse than others. Poets were often expected to confine their expression of feeling and ideas not only to the limitations of such external forms as the epic, sonnet, or ode (not to mention the demands of meter and rhyme), but also to use only words which were considered appropriate and dignified. Hence, the concept of poetic diction, a language of poetry, developed.

Students will easily detect the differences in style between poets such as Alexander Pope and Robert Frost. It may take some additional work with words to differentiate what happens in poems by Pope and Keats, Frost and Plath.

Procedure

1. Distribute **Handout 25.** Students should reexamine the poems indicated, refer to The Poetry Analysis Worksheet (**Handout 21**), and be prepared to provide examples which support their conclusions. After they have had some time to work on the handout, discuss the diction of these poems with the class. In order to allow for sufficient discussion time, you may wish to ask students to complete this worksheet before class begins.

Suggested Responses:

"Sound and Sense" (Pope): The language is very formal, replete with mythical allusions which are molded into metaphorical illustrations of the major theme: "The sound must seem an echo to the sense." The word choice, although not pretentious, reflects the formal tone (as does the often inverted syntax): "Tis not enough no harshness gives offense." With the exception of the allusions, most words are abstract (art, chance, harshness, sound, sense, etc.) with very little emphasis on connotation.

"Out, Out—" (Frost): The informal, conversational style of the poem is realized by the choice of very simple words and a very concrete, dramatized situation. The poem also takes full advantage of the emotional expectations of the reader ("big boy/Doing a man's work, though a child at heart") without being sentimental.

"Ode on a Grecian Urn" (Keats): In many ways more formal than even Pope's couplets, with a hint of classical allusion throughout, yet never specified, this ode reflects all of the conventionality of its form. It employs the abstractions of apostrophe, yet has all of the concrete sensual detail and emotional resonance of the most intimate of lyrics.

"Daddy" (Plath): The conversational style, although informal, is constrained by the somewhat stylized lines and singsong rhythms. The vocabulary is commonplace, although the highly connotative allusions to Hitler and the Jews need some explanation. The descriptions are so specific (even personal) that they may appear obscure, e.g., the reference to her husband, "a man in black with a Meinkamp look," whom she modeled after her father. Various colloquial or slang terms also contribute to the informal quality of the poem (e.g., "Daddy," "gobbledygoo," "panzer-man," "stuck me together").

79

2. Distribute **Handout 26.** This exercise may be completed in class or assigned for homework.

Suggested Responses:

1. *Critics are more impressed by obscurity than significance, techniques rather than teachings.*

2. *realistic/negative:*

carnage	*death*
blood	*face down*
murder	*cold Korean mud*
lynch	*discontent*
working out her guts	*plaintive whimper*
whine	
rebellion	

3. *pleasant/positive:*

mild and gracious	*lavender*
pale	*dreamy*
glory	*money*
wan	*refined*
effervescent jive	*alive*
melody	*subtle*
autumn leaf	

4. *By his sardonic use of words which typically have positive/pleasant connotations, he has deviously obscured their associations and juxtaposed them with the negative/realistic experiences of life, creating a level of irony throughout the poem.*

5. *allusion: to the Korean war and the negative socio-economic experiences of many black people*

   slang: "working out her guts"; "he ain't"; "corny"

   metaphor/concrete detail: ". . . an autumn leaf hanging from a tree—I see a body!"

   abstract words: obscure, devious, imagery, rebellion

6. *Poetry should not obscure the facts, finding deceptive words for hiding some of the unpleasant realities of life. The poem that is "obscure" and "subtle" is not telling the truth.*

Name _____

Date _____

Dealing with Diction

Examine the following poems from previous handouts. Taking into account various figures of speech, allusions, use of slang, "sophisticated" vocabulary, abstract words, concrete words, and highly connotative words, comment on the diction of each poem. Be sure to indicate whether the diction is formal or informal.

"Sound and Sense" (Pope):

"Out, Out—" (Frost):

"Ode on a Grecian Urn" (Keats):

"Daddy" (Plath):

"Mild and Gracious Words"

Read the following poem and, after a careful examination of its diction, answer the questions which follow it.

I Know I'm Not Sufficiently Obscure

I know I'm not sufficiently obscure
to please the critics—nor devious enough.
Imagery escapes me.
I cannot find those mild and gracious words
to clothe the carnage.   5
Blood is blood and murder's murder.
What's a lavender word for lynch?
Come, you pale poets, wan, refined and dreamy:
here is a black woman working out her guts
in a white man's kitchen   10
for little money and no glory.
How should I tell that story?
There is a black boy, blacker still from death,
face down in the cold Korean mud.
Come on with your effervescent jive   15
explain to him why he ain't alive.
Reword our specific discontent
into some plaintive melody,
a little whine, a little whimper,
not too much—and no rebellion!   20
God, no! Rebellion's much too corny.
You deal with finer feelings,
very subtle—an autumn leaf
hanging from a tree—I see a body!

—Ray Durem

1. What is the speaker's attitude toward critics?

2. What words in the poem were perhaps chosen for their realistic/negative connotations?

3. What words in the poem were perhaps chosen for their pleasant/positive connotations?

4. How has the author made use of these two categories of words in relation to each other?

5. Cite examples of:

   a. allusion

   b. slang

   c. metaphor

   d. concrete detail

   e. abstract words

6. In view of what the poem "means," what would you suspect are the poet's views about the "purpose" of poetry?

Lesson 13

"Endowed with Energy": Imagery

Objective

- To explore the role of imagery in the development of poetic discourse

Notes to the Teacher

The imagistic movement in poetry was a reaction to the tendency to generalize, moralize, and sentimentalize in much romantic and Victorian poetry. The movement, which had a tremendous impact on the development of modern poetry during the first few decades of the twentieth century, opposed abstraction. Ezra Pound, one of the early leaders of the group, helped to formulate the guidelines:

1. The "thing," whether subjective or objective, must be treated directly.

2. No word is to be used which does not contribute to the presentation.

3. The rhythm must be an echo of the musical phrase of words (cadence), not that of a metronome (meter).

Pound then went on to define an "image" as "that which presents an intellectual and emotional complex in an instant of time." Later he stated: "It is a vortex or cluster of fused ideas and is endowed with energy." But as Jacob Issacs points out in his *Backgrounds of Modern Poetry* (chapter 3, "The Coming of the Image"):

> Imagism is not the facile presentation of images or pictures; it is hard, clear, unblurred statement, whether it uses metaphor or not. It must be done by means of the chosen 'exact word. . . which brings the effect of that object before the reader as it presented itself to the poet's mind at the time of writing the poem.[1] (Aldington) It is the hard sculptural quality which marks off the best Imagist work, even if the tension, the dwelling upon a point of excitement, cannot be maintained for long.

Although the "image" is certainly not new to poetry prior to the twentieth century, the imagistic movement has been a major influence in altering the entire process of poetic expression. Contemporary poets and readers are sensitive to the energizing potential of a well chosen image. When Ezra Pound defined poetry as "language charged with meaning," he used an electronic metaphor true to the times as well as to the text. Although it is necessary for the reader to plug into the poem and turn on the switch, modern poetry is especially accessible if students become sensitive to the ways that poetry is "endowed with energy."

Procedure

1. Distribute **Handout 27.** Students may complete this worksheet in advance or during class in small groups or large groups. Answers will vary, but some examples from previous handouts include the following:

Sight: "Outside in the road the telegraph wire
    to the town from the darkening land
Intones to travellers like a spectral lyre
    swept by a spectral hand.:

(Hardy's "Nobody Comes," **Handout 10**)

Sound: "The buzz-saw snarled and rattled in the yard. . ."

(Frost's "Out, Out—," **Handout 2**)

Touch: "Sometimes I feel so weak I just want to explode
Explode and tear this town apart
Take a knife and cut this pain from my heart."

(Springsteen's "The Promised Land," **Handout 15**)

Students will be hard pressed to draw on specific images of taste and smell from the handouts at this point. Ask them to be alert for examples in lessons which follow.

2. Distribute **Handout 28.** These poems provide the opportunity for students to experience various ways in which imagery is effectively employed.

Suggested Responses:

1. *The sight and sound images generate a time contrast.*

2. *The images contrast with one another. The images move from "what seemed so far away" (the moon), to what is "near" (midnight/moon), to what is "imagined" ("child's balloon").*

3. *The title is deceptive. The contrasts are either stated or implied: body without beauty/body with beauty; river/dish water; street/palm trees.*

4. *The various images create an atmosphere of an unpleasant place. However, the personified images alter the tone to one of humor, e.g., "Shoots. . . Lolling obscenely" and a "congress of stinks."*

5. *This couplet is entirely abstract and nonimagistic.*

Name _____

Date _____

Imagery: "Endowed with Energy"

A poem very often depends on the sense appeal of words in order to recreate the quality of experience which the poet wishes the reader to feel and think about. Recall your experiences of previously-read poems, and cite phrases or lines which you feel were particularly effective in communicating sense experience. Indicate your sources. If you cannot discover examples of specific senses appealed to, create your own.

Sense Appealed to	*Quote/Source*
Sight	
Taste	
Smell	
Sound	
Touch	

Imagine This

Directions: Underline the words in the following which have the most imagistic effect. Discuss the different ways in which the imagery is handled.

1. Old houses were scaffolding once
        and workmen whistling.

                                    —T. E. Hulme

2. Above the quiet dock at midnight,
    Tangled in the tall mast's corded height,
    Hangs the moon. What seemed so far away
    Is but a child's balloon, forgotten after play.

                                    —T. E. Hulme

3.   No Images

        She does not know
        Her beauty,
        She thinks her brown body
        Has no glory.

        If she could dance   5
        Naked,
        Under palm trees.
        And see her image in the river
        She would know.

        But there are no palm trees   10
        On the street,
        And dish water gives back no images.

                                    —Waring Cuney

4.   Root Cellar

    Nothing would sleep in that cellar, dank as a ditch.
    Bulbs broke out of boxes hunting for chinks in the dark,
    Shoots dangled and drooped,
    Lolling obscenely from mildewed crates,
    Hung down long yellow evil necks, like tropical snakes.   5
    And what a congress of stinks!—
    Roots ripe as old bait,
    Pulpy stems, rank, silo-rich,
    Leaf-mold, manure, lime, piled against slippery planks.
    Nothing would give up life: 10
    Even the dirt kept breathing a small breath.

                                        —Theodore Roethke

5. 'Tis not enough no harshness gives offense,
   The sound must seem an echo to the sense.

                                        —Alexander Pope

Lesson 14

"Very Like a Whale": The Metaphorical Mind

Objective

- To explore the ways in which the imagination expands upon experience

Notes to the Teacher

The figurative leap into the unknown territory of the imagination is both easy and difficult for students. Their early experience of literature is often based on a world of "make believe" and "let's pretend." Childhood fantasy literature very often proceeds from this premise; it does not fluctuate so much between "the real" and "the imagined." The world of Cinderella, Jack and the Beanstalk, and Mickey Mouse is not the world of the playground down the street, the friend next door, and mother in the next room.

Metaphoric language demands that we relate to the real and the imagined at the same time, but often in complex ways. Although metaphor is embedded in the clichés of everyday speech, it is often examined and colloquial (therefore, learned by repetition and not by the imagination). It is only a very young child who would be fascinated and entertained by the statement that it is "raining cats and dogs." Consequently, since so many students approach poetry with a programmed imagination and a scientific respect for facts, one of the major tasks of an AP teacher is to provide students with opportunities to mistrust what the words of a poem seem to be saying. As Robert Frost has warned: "Poetry provides the one permissible way of saying one thing and meaning another."

Procedure

1. Distribute **Handout 29.** Discuss the brief passage from *Hamlet* which establishes the context for a discussion of metaphor, leading to an examination of Nash's "Very Like a Whale." Use the discussion questions which follow each selection.

Suggested Responses:

Passage 1: Hamlet, III. 2:376–381

1. *He does not actually see them, of course, unless he is mad. He sees similarities in shapes. Also, he may be engaging in a "put on" with Polonius.*

2. *Either Polonius does have the imagination to see the similarity or he is trying to conciliate Hamlet, whom he considers to be mad. Those students who are familiar with the play will remember that the latter is true.*

Passage 2: "Very Like a Whale," Nash

1. *So that poems will be more literal, make better "sense" and be "true to fact."*

2. *The speaker chooses a literal interpretation and ignores the metaphorical context in which "The Assyrian," referring to King Sennacherib, is a synecdoche, the substitution of a part (King Sennacherib) for the whole (the Assyrian army).*

3. *The wolf had "purple and gold" cohorts; that Byron thought that King Sennacherib was a wolf (and the speaker wants definite proof); that people will follow his literal interpretation and think of Old Testament soldiers who were devoured by wolves; that "the snow is a white blanket" is a false statement (and this can be proven).*

4. *Most students will argue that the humorous tone of the poem, established by the ludicrous, literal interpretations of the speaker and the outrageous rhymes, supports the idea that the poet is playing around with language himself. This imaginative idea and word play is itself poetry. Ogden Nash (or his "voice" in this poem) has no real prejudices against Byron and poets from Homer to the present who use "too much metaphor and simile."*

2. Ask students why Nash's poem title is appropriate. Would "Very Like a Fox" have served his purpose as well?

Suggested Response:

By alluding to the line "Very like a whale" in Hamlet, Nash has made the most of a humorous context. At the point when Polonius delivers this line he is attempting to conciliate Hamlet whom he considers mad. Nash, in a humorous vein, is demonstrating how a poet's metaphorical "madness," if taken literally, can also result in a form of reader madness.

The Metaphorical Mind: Very Like a Whale

Directions: Read the following selections and answer the questions for each.

Passage 1: *Hamlet*, III, 2:376–381

The following dialogue from Shakespeare's *Hamlet* is between Prince Hamlet (who is either mad or pretends to be mad) and Polonius, the Lord Chamberlain.

> Hamlet: Do you see yonder cloud that's almost in shape of a camel?
> Polonius: By th' mass, and 'tis like a camel, indeed.
> Hamlet: Methinks it is like a weasel.
> Polonius: It is back'd like a weasel.
> Hamlet: Or like a whale.
> Polonius: Very like a whale.

1. Why does Hamlet see so many different kinds of animals in a cloud?

2. Why does Polonius agree with Hamlet?

Passage 2:

Very Like a Whale

One thing that literature would be greatly the better for
Would be a more restricted employment by authors of simile and
    metaphor.
Authors of all races, be they Greeks, Romans, Teutons or Celts,
Can't seem just to say that anything is the thing it is but have to go
    out of their way to say that it is like something else.
What does it mean when we are told
That the Assyrian came down like a wolf on the fold?   5
In the first place, George Gordon Byron had had enough experience
To know that it probably wasn't just one Assyrian, it was a *lot* of
    Assyrians.

However, as too many arguments are apt to induce apoplexy and
    thus hinder longevity,
We'll let it pass as one Assyrian for the sake of brevity.   10
Now then, this particular Assyrian, the one whose cohorts were
    gleaming in purple and gold,
Just what does the poet mean when he says he came down like a
    wolf on the fold?
In heaven and earth more than is dreamed of in our philosophy there
    are a great many things,
But I don't imagine that among them there is a wolf with purple and
    gold cohorts or purple and gold anythings.
No, no, Lord Byron, before I'll believe that this Assyrian was actually
    like a wolf I must have some kind of proof;
Did he run on all fours and did he have a hairy tail and a big red
    mouth and big white teeth and did he say Woof woof woof?
Frankly I think it very unlikely, and all you were entitled to say, at
    the very most,
Was that the Assyrian cohorts came down like a lot of Assyrian cohorts
    about to destroy the Hebrew host.
But that wasn't fancy enough for Lord Byron, oh dear me, no, he had
    to invent a lot of figures of speech and then interpolate them,
With the result that whenever you mention Old Testament soldiers to
    people they say Oh yes, they're the ones that a lot of wolves dressed
    up in gold and purple ate them.
That's the kind of thing that's being done all the time by poets, from
    Homer to Tennyson;
They're always comparing ladies to lilies and veal to venison,
And they always say things like that the snow is a white blanket after
    a winter storm.
Oh it is, is it, all right then, you sleep under a six-inch blanket of
    snow and I'll sleep under a half-inch blanket of unpoetical
    blanket material and we'll see which one keeps warm,
And after that maybe you'll begin to comprehend dimly
What I mean by too much metaphor and simile.

—Ogden Nash

1. Why does the speaker advocate a "more restricted employment" of simile and metaphor?

2. What is the basis for misunderstanding Byron's use of "the Assyrian"?

3. What are some of the other "misreadings" of metaphor that the speaker uses?

4. Do you feel that the speaker wants to be taken seriously? Why or why not?

Lesson 15
Serpents and Ice Cream: The Ways of Metaphor

Objective

• To demonstrate a variety of ways in which the metaphorical mind can manipulate meaning for greater effect

Notes to the Teacher

Traditional rhetoricians have categorized and labeled over two-hundred figures of speech. Handbooks have been produced, intended to guide students to write and speak with flair and style once the basics (logic and grammar) were mastered. Most of these figures are in some way variations on metaphor, ways of stating similarity. Finding the similarities between human and nonhuman things is a basic activity of the metaphorical mind. Primitive societies often developed religious beliefs based on animism or phychism. Ancient poets went on to develop a body of literature, mythology, based on the contrasting tendency, anthropomorphism. In both efforts, the imagination attempted to personify, to reduce to its own terms, what was nonhuman, either subhuman or superhuman.

In some modes of expression, the inanimate is addressed as though it were animate. This figurative convention we identify as apostrophe. However, students should be warned that this figure also can be used as direct address to a person as though present or to the dead as though living. Likewise, an invocation to the gods or the muses, or a prayer to the saints or to the Deity, is a form of apostrophe.

Departing from similarities, the metaphorical mind will often focus on a comparison or contrast of differences. When a poet engages in hyperbole or understatement, the purpose is usually to emphasize the discrepancy between what is and what is not. Cummings highlights the differences between mankind and nature in "when serpents bargain for the right to squirm" in completely hyperbolic terms. Wallace Stevens, on the other hand, understates his meaning in "The Emperor of Ice Cream."

The difficulty or the challenge in reading any metaphorical statement is to bring the flight of fancy in for a safe landing and to realize the reason for the journey in the first place.

Procedure

1. Distribute **Handout 30.** You may wish students to complete Part I prior to class or in small groups.

Some Possible Responses:

Personification:

Handout 1: . . . multi-coloured multi-minded
United beautiful States of terrible America

("Norman Morrison"
—Mitchell)

Handout 2: . . . At the word, the saw
As if to prove saws knew what supper meant,
Leaped out at the boy's hand. . .

("Out, Out—" —Frost)

Understatement:

Handout 2: . . . The boy saw all . . .
He saw all spoiled . . .

("Out, Out—" —Frost)

Handout 27: But there are no palm trees
On the street,
And dish water gives back no images.

("No Images" —Cuney)

Apostrophe:

Handout 7: In the poem "Daddy" by Sylvia Plath, the speaker addresses a dead father.

Handout 12: In Keat's "Ode on a Grecian Urn," the speaker directly addresses the urn itself.

Hyperbole:

Handout 7:　　*"Daddy, I have had to kill you . . .*
a bag full of God. . ."

("Daddy" —Plath)

2. Read the poems in Part II with the students. Ask them to deal with their initial confusion by attempting to state a tentative theme for each poem. Then, working in either small groups or together as a class, read each poem carefully and circle or underline parts of it which need to be explained in terms of the proposed theme.

Suggested Clarifications:

"when serpents bargain for the right to squirm"

The poem satirizes human beings by suggesting that even animals do not engage in some of the activities of "unanimal mankind." In addition to the images of contrast between nature and human nature, the poem also communicates a distaste for

a. organized labor: to bargain for rights; to strike

b. bureaucratic incongruities: The unpleasant things in life (thorns) are threatened by the pleasant (roses); the promise of reward (rainbow) must be "insured" (e.g., social security).

c. Art (thrush's song) is controlled by the majority, those who are considered the wisest and who "make the most noise" (screech owls).

d. bureaucratic formalities/control: "sign on the dotted line"; "permission"; accusations and denouncements

"The Emperor of Ice-Cream"

In one of his letters to an inquiring editor concerning the meaning of this poem, Stevens wrote:

It may or may not be like converting a piece of mysticism into a piece of logic.

As Milton Bates points out in Wallace Stevens: A Mythology of Self (University of California Press, Berkley, 1985):

It was not a question of mystification. Rather, he understood that pure poetry succeeds when it detaches the reader from reason and reality and lifts him by the most tenuous of threads to make the reader overly conscious of those filaments and so subvert their function.

By pure poetry, Stevens made a distinction between the "true subject" and the "poetry of the subject." In "The Emperor of Ice-Cream" the subject is the death of an old woman (her room, her corpse, those who gather to wake her). The poetic attitude becomes prominent, however, and the subject is deemphasized somewhat as certain details, imaginatively conceived, reflect "the poetry of the subject."

The Mourners: "The roller of big cigars/The muscular one" (capitalist? opportunist? life itself?) is like a carnival barker, implying that life and the ritual of death are something of a sideshow. The "wenches. . .dress/As they are used to wear" ("wenches" connotes "easy virtue"; implication is that there should be no "dressing up" of death, which is an ordinary, routine event). "Boys/Bring flowers (beauty) in last month's newspapers" (truth, facts).

The Ritual: Ice cream (equated with "concupiscent curds") seems to be what life is all about, its sweetness. "Embroidered fantails" cover what is. An ironic detail, the birds are symbolic of beauty, freedom, life. "The lamp" (showing what is) is focused on the "horny feet" of the corpse, not on what covers it. Life is stored in a "dresser" with knobs missing.

The Deceased: What is is without glamour ("horny feet," "cold," "dumb").

Name _____

Date _____

The Ways of Metaphor

Part I: Based on your understanding, give examples of the following figures of speech from previously studied poems.

1. Personification

2. Understatement

3. Apostrophe

4. Hyperbole

Part II: Read the following poems and circle or underline parts which pose problems of interpretation. Make marginal notes and be prepared to ask questions and offer observations during a discussion.

when serpents bargain for the right to squirm

when serpents bargain for the right to squirm
and the sun strikes to gain a living wage—
when thorns regard their roses with alarm
and rainbows are insured against old age

when every thrush may sing no new moon in
if all screech-owls have not okayed his voice
—and any wave signs on the dotted line
or else an ocean is compelled to close

when the oak begs permission of the birch
to make an acorn—valleys accuse their
mountains of having altitude—and march
denounces april as a saboteur

then we'll believe in that incredible
unanimal mankind (and not until)

—E. E. Cummings

The Emperor of Ice-Cream

Call the roller of big cigars,
The muscular one, and bid him whip
In kitchen cups concupiscent curds.
Let the wenches dawdle in such dress
As they are used to wear, and let the boys
Bring flowers in last month's newspapers.
Let be be finale of seem.
The only emperor is the emperor of ice-cream.

Take from the dresser of deal,
Lacking the three glass knobs, that sheet
On which she embroidered fantails once
And spread it so as to cover her face.
If her horny feet protrude, they come
To show how cold she is, and dumb.
Let the lamp affix its beam.
The only emperor is the emperor of ice-cream

—Wallace Stevens

Lesson 16

The Ring and the Bird in the Storm: Symbolism

Objectives

- To examine, analyze, and interpret symbols in poetry
- To differentiate various levels of meaning within a poem: the literal, metaphorical, and symbolical

Notes to the Teacher

Language is symbolic. Words refer to or stand for objects. Just as we use certain objects to bear the weight of more meaning (flag, cross, red light), so the poet depends on certain words in certain contexts to amplify meaning. In Adrian Mitchell's poem, "Norman Morrison," we do not hesitate to accept the literal "facts" of the case. This is about a man who set himself on fire at a certain time, in a certain place, and, we assume, for the reasons indicated.

The poem also states that

He simply burned away his clothes,
his passport, his pink-tinted skin,
put on a new skin of flame
and became
Vietnamese.

We assume that the last three lines of this passage, following the understatement of the first two ("simply"), are to be taken metaphorically. And finally, after all is accounted for, we might consider Norman Morrison the man as a symbol of resistance to the United States' involvement in Vietnam. The action, self-immolation, is now symbolic of the Vietnamese people killed in the crossfire of a war. The place is suddenly symbolic: "outside the Pentagon . . . in Washington where everyone could see" (In contrast to the "the dark corners of Vietnam where nobody could see"). Even the time of year is symbolic (the fall in the "multi-colored . . . United . . . States," suggesting the colors of the season, as well as racial diversity). An argument can even be made for the choice of days, or perhaps this is just ironic. November 2 is All Souls Day in the Christian calendar, a day of prayer for the souls of those suffering in pur-

gatorial fires in order to be purified for their acceptance into heaven.

These three levels of response, the literal, metaphorical, and symbolical, are ways in which the reader becomes more engaged in the layers of significance which a poem can incorporate. Of course, students invariably ask: Did the poet know what he was doing? Did she mean that? Did she intend for readers to get all of this out of the poem? Our answer must be "Yes" and "No." The poet did intend to create a work of art, to accept the challenge of doing many different and difficult things well at the same time if they were suited to the poem. The poet probably did not intend (at least consciously) all of the interpretations which an analysis yields, but, since readers seldom have access to a poet's intentions, they are on their own. Their interaction with the poem provides them with the only meaning that it has to offer short of accepting unquestioningly the interpretations of others.

Students, of course, immediately interpret this position as a triumph for subjectivity. A poem can now mean what we want it to mean! Not true! Would "Norman Morrison" be the same poem if it were about a man who escaped from a mental institution and set himself on fire on April 1, 1988 in Pittsburgh? The interpretation of a poem must emerge from the text and the reader at the same time. When either is inadequate, the response to the experience is incomplete.

Procedure

1. Review levels of meaning with students, utilizing Adrian Mitchell's poem "Norman Morrison" (**Handout 1**) and the above notes. Any other poem that illustrates literal, metaphorical, and symbolic levels could also serve this purpose.

2. Discuss the concept of poet's intention and its relevance to critical response. Use the above notes as a theoretical basis, but re-

late the theory to a specific poem such as Mitchell's "Norman Morrison."

3. Distribute **Handout 31.** Although students may have already dealt with the various levels of meaning in their study of some of the poems on previous handouts, this exercise provides them with a sense of how meaning often "builds" organically within a poem.

Suggested Responses:
1. a. "all" that had happened to his hand
   b. "All" of his life is "spoiled" just as his body (as his blood spills).
   c. "All" that has occurred stands for the fragility of life and when the boy "saw all" it is a moment of recognition for him.
2. a. It is a useless garden tool.
   b. It is meaningful in the context of life as a garden that needs to be cultivated. In this context, the "broken hoe" (like the "cold earth") is anything that interferes with life's fruition.
   c. It stands for anything which interferes with the natural development of things, as when justice is denied.
3. a. It stands for a medium of communication.
   b. It is like the strings of a harp, "a spectral lyre."
   c. It stands for communication or rather, for the speaker, a lack of it. It provides a connection with the town but the isolated speaker concludes that it—and everything relating to society—"has nothing to do with me."

4. Distribute **Handout 32.** Students could complete this activity in small groups or as homework. Use the completed worksheet as the basis for a discussion.

Suggested Responses:

Part I
1. a. time
   b. faith/a weight/stability
   c. long-term piety and devotion
   d. a telescope for looking above the earth
   e. sorrow, suffering
   f. an unready harvest
   g. a circle of completeness, perfection; marriage, fidelity

2. Hope stays around but its presence is somewhat purposeless.
3. The speaker wants to gain Hope's favor, but Hope is not easily controlled or won over.
4. The speaker's gifts are all efforts to promote self-worth, telling Hope in effect: "I have been pious and suffered much. It is time for you to unite yourself with me." Hope, on the other hand, returns gifts which tell the speaker to remain faithful, look beyond the here and now, and wait until it is time to be rewarded.

Part II
1. a. freedom/joy
   b. spirit or soul; spiritual; that which cannot be put into words, the incommunicable
   c. difficult times; difficult circumstances, places, and situations
   d. a small means of subsistence

2. Hope is comforting and joyful; it endures in spite of all obstacles and is self-sufficient.
3. It is "the thing with feathers . . . that kept so many warm." Unlike the other elements which pose a threat (air/ "the Gale . . . the storm"; earth/ "the chillest land"; water/"the strangest sea"), hope is self-sustained by fire (warmth), symbolic of both passion and purification, and does not need "a crumb" from the person in whose soul it "perches."

Part III

In Herbert's "Hope," image and metaphor merge into symbol. The gift-giving which occurs is metaphorical as is the anticipated "marriage" ("I did expect a ring.") Hope personified is compared to a loiterer, someone who is present but for no worthwhile purpose. However, the gifts are symbolic and, as a result, the act of exchange itself becomes symbolic.

The speaker tries to bribe Hope into a fulfillment of expectations. Hope, in contrast, is evasive, and symbolically reminds the speaker to endure patiently.

In Dickinson's poem, hope is ever-present and faithful, a source of consolation and joy. The nature of the relationship is very different. Herbert portrays it as a one-sided courting, resulting in unrequited love. The speaker, in Dickinson's terms, tries to give a "crumb" in order to sustain hope. Dickinson describes hope almost as though it were a pet which is always faithful but does not demand anything in return. As a result, both poems portray hope symbolically in very different ways. It is something that is evasive yet offers encouragement in Herbert's poem. It is constant and enduring in Dickinson's.

Name _____

Date _____

On the Level

Directions: Use various handouts and answer the following questions concerning literal, metaphorical, and symbolical meaning in poems.

1. In "Out, Out—" (**Handout 2**), what is meant in context by: "Then the boy saw all—"?

   a. literally

   b. metaphorically

   c. symbolically

2. In "Justice Denied in Massachusetts," (**Handout 4**), what does the "broken hoe" signify?

   a. literally

   b. metaphorically

   c. symbolically

3. What does "the telegraph wire" stand for in "Nobody Comes" (**Handout 10**)?

   a. literally

   b. metaphorically

   c. symbolically

Name _____

Date _____

The Ring and the Bird in the Storm

Part I
Directions: Read the following poem and answer the questions.

Hope

I gave to Hope a watch of mine: but he
    An anchor gave to me.
Then an old prayer-book I did present:
    And he an optic sent.
With that I gave a vial full of tears:
    But he a few green ears.
Ah loiterer! I'll no more, no more I'll bring:
    I did expect a ring.

—George Herbert

1. What symbolism would you attach to the following objects in the context of the poem?

   a. watch

   b. anchor

   c. prayer book

   d. optic

   e. vial of tears

   f. green ears

   g. ring

2. Why does the speaker call Hope a "loiterer"?

3. What is symbolized by the exchange of gifts between the speaker and Hope?

4. What do the speaker's gifts all have in common?

Part II

Directions: Read the following poem and answer the questions.

Hope Is the Thing with Feathers

Hope is the thing with feathers
That perches in the soul.
And sings the tune without the words
And never stops at all.

And sweetest in the gale is heard:
And sore must be the storm
That could abash the little bird
That kept so many warm.

I've heard it in the chillest land,
And on the strangest sea:
Yet, never, in extremity,
It asked a crumb of me.

—Emily Dickinson

1. What symbolism would you attach to the following in the context of Emily Dickinson's poem?

    a. a thing with feathers/little bird

    b. a tune without words

    c. a gale/storm; chillest land; strangest sea

    d. a crumb

2. What qualities of hope are noted by the speaker?

3. Other than "the little bird" and its "tune without words," how is hope symbolized?

Part III

Directions: In two or three well-developed and well-supported paragraphs, compare and contrast the ways that Herbert's and Dickinson's poems function on the metaphorical and symbolical levels.

Lesson 17
Wayfarers Working in the World: Allegory

Objective

- To examine, analyze and interpret allegory

Notes to the Teacher

Students will quickly note that some poems function on at least two levels at the same time. Herbert's "Hope," for example, would be intelligible as a courtship poem if the gifts exchanged were not so bizarre. If the objects were more conventional (letters, flowers, candy), then the poem could be allegorical. But those kinds of symbols would not have served the poet's purpose, communicating his insights on the nature of the relationship between hope and humanity. However, in some poems, such as those on the handouts for this lesson, the literal and the symbolic levels of the poem are consistent. There is a one-to-one correspondence between both levels of meaning. Allegory is, in a sense, a level of philosophical fantasy that can be explicated only after the symbols have been arranged and revealed by the contexts of the poem.

Procedure

1. Distribute **Handout 33**. Read the poems with the students and ask them to consider the use of symbolism in each. Specific questions have not been included on the handout in order to motivate students to start formulating their own questions and establishing their own focus in response to a poem. Some questions and observations which should surface are summarized here. It may be necessary to direct some of the questioning process.
   In General
   a. How do these poems communicate on the symbolic level more than on the literal? On the literal level all of the poems deal with specific, dramatized experiences: a journey, work activity, and a varied encounter with "the world and all her train." The details of the experience, however, suggest a more than literal interpretation, e.g., ". . . each weed . . . Was a singular knife."
   b. How do these poems differ in the use of symbolical meaning from those on **Handout 32** (Herbert's "Hope" and Dickinson's "Hope is a Thing with Feathers")? The poems in **Handout 32** use their symbols consistently, but the details do not make much sense on just the literal level (e.g., a bird in the soul). Herbert's poem has allegorical characteristics although it is somewhat ludicrous on the literal level.

Specific Observations
"The Wayfarer"
   The journey of life is implied (along a pathway).
   The human race (wayfarer) is on that journey.
   The growth of weeds represents a lack of civilization or outright neglect.
   Weeds as knives suggest the dangers which are on "the road less travelled"; truth is not easily pursued.
   The speaker's decision to look for "other roads" indicates an unwillingness to pursue truth if it poses a threat.
"Many Workmen"
   The workmen are those people who see themselves as creative.
   The "huge ball of masonry" represents achievement, although its proportion and eventual lack of stability indicate some prideful presumption. The fact that it is a "huge ball" is suggestive of "a world," in which case the workmen are imitating God in an effort to create their own world.
   The "mountain-top" indicates a desire to show off their work to those below them (in the "valley"), suggestive of rash pride.
   That "they loved the thing" implies their attachment to material things and their unrestrained pride.

When "It moved" and "came upon them," some kind of ironic punishment is suggested, reducing them to "blood" and a "squeal," i.e., death and ineffectual protest.

"The World"

"Ring of pure and endless light": the symbol within the simile is traditional; a ring (perfection, unity, a world); light (grace, perfection, knowledge).

"the spheres": control time in motion

"her train": the world is personified as feminine and royal; her "train" consists of character types such as the "doting lover," the "miser," etc.

"lute" = "Wit's sour delights"; "gloves and knots" (i.e., trinkets such as a ribbon tied in a love knot) = "snares" or traps of pleasure

"flower" = a thing of natural beauty

"darksome stateman" = in the "kingdom of the World of eternity"; could be the devil or evil or the various other negative associations suggested, e.g., "moved like a thick midnight fog" or an underground mole that will "clutch his prey," sinners, and feed upon them

"the miser on a heap of dust" = all who are obsessed with possessing the material things of this life that will eventually become "rust" and "dust"

(This is perhaps a veiled allusion to the New Testament passage which encourages us to gather treasures in heaven rather than here on earth. The miser, however, "would not place one piece above.")

the "epicure" = all who are enslaved by physical pleasure

"some, who . . . did weep and sing" = those who either repent or rejoice in their spiritual state but who are not admitted into the ring of light (heaven) from their "dark abode" (earth) because "the bridegroom did for none provide/ But for his bride" (Christ, the bridegroom, only admits those who are faithful to Him and His Church, the bride.) The symbolism of the bridegroom and the bride is derived from the *Song of Songs* of the Hebrew scriptures and has traditionally been given this allegorical interpretation by Christianity.

Wayfarers Working in the World

Directions: Read the following poems carefully and interpret their symbolism on an allegorical level; that is, establish a one-to-one correspondence between the literal and symbolic levels so that both communicate a consistent level of meaning whereby all of the symbols bear a relationship to each other. Circle those words or phrases in each poem which you feel provide the clues to a consistent allegorical interpretation. Provide a short statement after each poem which summarizes its allegorical meaning, based on your analysis of its network of symbols.

The Wayfarer

The wayfarer,
Perceiving the pathway to truth,
Was struck with astonishment.
It was thickly grown with weeds.
"Ha," he said,
"I see that none has passed here
In a long time."
Later he saw that each weed
Was a singular knife.
"Well," he mumbled at last,
"Doubtless there are other roads."

—Stephen Crane

Many Workmen

Many workmen
Built a huge ball of masonry
Upon a mountain-top.
Then they went to the valley below,

And turned to behold their work.
"It is grand," they said;
They loved the thing.

Of a sudden, it moved;
It came upon them swiftly;
It crushed them all to blood.
But some had opportunity to squeal.

—Stephen Crane

The World

I saw eternity the other night
Like a great ring of pure and endless light,
   All calm as it was bright;
And round beneath it, time in hours, days, years,
     Driv'n by the spheres

Like a vast shadow moved, in which the world
   And all her train were hurled;
The doting lover in his quaintest strain
     Did there complain;
Near him his lute, his fancy, and his flights,   10
     Wit's sour delights,
With gloves and knots, the silly snares of pleasure,
     Yet his dear treasure,
All scattered lay, while he his eyes did pore
     Upon a flower.

The darksome statesman, hung with weights and woe,
Like a thick midnight fog moved there so slow
   He did not stay, nor go;
Condemning thoughts, like sad eclipses, scowl
    Upon his soul,   20
And clouds of crying witnesses without
   Pursued him with one shout;
Yet digged the mole, and lest his ways be found
    Worked underground,
Where he did clutch his prey, but One did see
    That policy;
Churches and altars fed him; perjuries
    Were gnats and flies;
It rained about him blood and tears, but he
    Drank them as free.   30

The fearful miser on a heap of rust
Sat pining all his life there, did scarce trust
   His own hands with the dust.
Yet would not place one piece above, but lives
    In fear of thieves.
Thousands there were as frantic as himself,
   And hugged each one his pelf;
The downright epicure placed heav'n in sense,
    And scorned pretense;
While others, slipped into a wide excess,   40
    Said little less;
The weaker sort slight trivial wares enslave,
    Who think them brave;
And poor despised truth sat counting by
    Their victory.

Yet some, who all this while did weep and sing,
And sing and weep, soared up into the ring;
   But most would use no wing.
O fools, said I, thus to prefer dark night
    Before true light.   50
To live in grots and caves, and hate the day
   Because it shows the way,
The way which from this dead and dark abode
    Leads up to God.
A way where you might tread the sun, and be
    More bright than he.
But as I did their madness so discuss,
    One whispered thus:
This ring the bridegroom did for none provide
    But for his bride.   60

—Henry Vaughan

Lesson 18
Evaluation: "Easing the Spring"

Objectives

• To evaluate students' understanding and application of poetic theory
• To simulate the format and content of the poetry component of the Advanced Placement Examination in Literature and Composition

Notes to the Teacher

The Advanced Placement Examination in English Literature and Composition, which students will be expected to take in order to acquire college credit, is composed of two sections: objective and essay. The objective section consists of questions based on four-to-six selections of prose and poetry. Students usually have 75 minutes to complete this section, which is used as the basis for 40 percent of their grade. The essay section usually consists of three essays which students are expected to complete in 105 minutes.

Students should have multiple opportunities to take examinations which simulate the format and style of this test. The two-part examination for this lesson attempts such a simulation. Obviously, the time frame has been scaled down to the limitations of the typical testing time (a fifty-minute period).

Procedure

1. Administer the test (**Handout 34**) during one class period. Indicate at the beginning of the test that students are expected to complete the entire test and how much time should be dedicated to each section.

2. Answers: Part I (4 points each)
   1. e   3. a   5. e   7. c   9. a
   2. d   4. d   6. e   8. d   10. d

3. Suggested Response: Part II (60 points)

The student essay should touch on most of the elements considered in this sample essay.

The sonnet "Spring" is an exuberant hymn to the energy of nature and a religious insight into the nature of innocence from a Christian perspective. Many of the images of the octave depict action in their metaphorical development: "weeds" are like "wheels;" they also "shoot." The thrush's song does so "rinse and wring" that it "strikes like lightning." The lambs are "racing" and having "their fling." Other images depict an idealized porcelain nature. The thrush eggs are as blue as "heavens," and the "peartree leaves and blooms" are "glassy." All of the images portray a nature that is fertile.

The sestet expresses a metaphysical response to the question which nature inspires: Why? The answer alludes to Eden, when the earth's beginning was innocent spring ("Mayday") and a girl and boy (Adam and Eve) were of "innocent mind." The speaker warns, with almost a spiritualized *carpe diem*, that we must "Have, get, before it cloy. . . cloud. . . and sour with sinning." Perhaps there is a submerged allusion to the Christian scriptural admonition to "become as little children" in order to enter heaven, although Christ, a "maid's child," has already chosen us as "worthy the winning." Although "Mayday" could refer to the pagan fertility rites (in which case it would be used ironically), in the context it also suggests the Catholic custom of devotion to Mary, the Mother of Christ, as Queen of the May.

In addition to images of sight and sound, the multiple uses of alliteration (especially "l" and "sh" sounds) and assonance echo the vitality of nature which the poem describes.

4. The following rubric may be employed to score the essay holistically:

9–10: well written	differentiates the development in the octave and sestet
a complete analysis of the imagery	analyzes the use of allusion
relates images to figures of speech employed	analyzes the theme and relates the imagery to its development
makes note of the sonnet form	analyzes sound patterns as they are relevant to thematic development

Note: Any answer that does not fulfill most of these expectations should be rated as follows:

8. Very good (but deficient in several respects)

7. Good (but undeveloped and/or inaccurate in not considering all aspects of the text)

6. Inadequate (in its support and development)

5. Unacceptable (does not relate to the question)

The score out of ten points should be multiplied by six in order to weigh the answer as 60 percent of the composite score.

Total Score:

Objective Section ＿＿＿ (40 pts.)
Essay Section ＿＿＿ (60 pts.)
Total ＿＿＿ (100 pts.)

The Advanced Placement Examination is converted to a five-point scale. Although the procedure is somewhat different, you may indicate to students that the following scale reflects their level of performance:
5 = 93-100 4 = 85-92 3 = 75-84
2 = 70-74 1 = 60-69

Unit Examination

Part I: Read the following poem and select the best answer to each question. (15 minutes)

Naming of Parts

Today we have naming of parts. Yesterday,
We had daily cleaning. And tomorrow morning,
We shall have what to do after firing. But today,
Today we have naming of parts. Japonica
5   Glistens like coral in all of the neighboring gardens,
    And today we have naming of parts.

This is the lower sling swivel. And this
Is the upper sling swivel, whose use you will see,
When you are given your slings. And this is the piling swivel,
10   Which in your case you have not got. The branches
Hold in the gardens their silent, eloquent gestures,
    Which in our case we have not got.

This is the safety-catch, which is always released
With an easy flick of the thumb. And please do not let me
15   See anyone using his finger. You can do it quite easy
If you have any strength in your thumb. The blossoms
Are fragile and motionless, never letting anyone see
    Any of them using their finger.

And this you can see is the bolt. The purpose of this
20   Is to open the breech, as you see. We can slide it
Rapidly backwards and forwards: we call this
Easing the spring. And rapidly backwards and forwards
The early bees are assaulting and fumbling the flowers:
    They call it easing the Spring.

25   They call it easing the Spring: it is perfectly easy
If you have any strength in your thumb: like the bolt,
And the breech, and the cocking-piece, and the point of balance,
Which in our case we have not got; and the almond-blossom
Silent in all of the gardens and the bees going backwards and forwards,
    For today we have naming of parts.

—Henry Reed

1. In the context of the entire poem, the speaker is

   a. a gardener   b. an observer
   c. a religious person   d. a botanist
   e. a military person

2. The poem is unified by all except one of the following:

   a. time: an emphasis on the present
   b. the contrast between the military activity and the activity in nature
   c. the use of six-line stanzas
   d. the use of a consistent meter and rhyme scheme
   e. the use of repetition

3. The most ironic aspect of the poem is

   a. the contrast between the military activity directed toward death and the coming to life of everything in nature
   b. the abstract, generalized statements of the speaker and the concrete, specific descriptions of nature
   c. the literal and metaphorical levels which are developed simultaneously
   d. the play on words evident in the use of "parts" and "easing the spring"
   e. the use of *carpe diem* theme

4. The title "Naming of Parts" is repeated in various contexts throughout the poem. It is used in all except one of the following ways:

   a. in a literal sense, in reference to the parts of a gun
   b. in a metaphorical sense, in reference to nature
   c. in a symbolic sense, in reference to the mental activity of the speaker in describing the "parts" of a gun and of nature
   d. in an allegorical sense, in reference to the personifications of war and nature
   e. in a rhetorical sense, with repetition for transition and emphasis

5. Similarities and differences between the military images and those in nature are evident in all but one of the following:

   a. the well-cleaned gun and the japonica which glistens
   b. the "silent, eloquent gestures" of the branches in the garden and the "all thumbs" clumsiness ascribed to the young soldiers
   c. the "easing the spring/Spring" activities of the soldiers and the bees
   d. the incomplete, almost sterile quality of the soldiers who do not have "piling swivels" and the bees who are "assaulting and fumbling the flowers"
   e. the evocation of symbols of potential evil in the bees

6. The setting for the poem perhaps serves a symbolic function:

   a. as an allusion to World War II
   b. by providing a contrast to urban living
   c. as an obvious allusion to the garden of Eden
   d. by contributing to the ecological theme
   e. by demonstrating that nature is not diminished or affected by the machinations of mankind

7. The shift of diction in the poem is evident

   a. in the middle of the third stanza
   b. in the last line of each stanza
   c. when the speaker describes the details of the "neighboring-gardens"
   d. in the use of puns
   e. by the repetition of certain key phrases

8. All of the following phrases from the poem are figurative except

   a. "Japonica/Glistens like coral. . ."
   b. "The branches/Hold in the gardens their silent, eloquent gestures. . ."
   c. "the blossoms. . . never letting anyone see/Any of them using their finger."
   d. ". . .We call this/Easing the spring."
   e. "The early bees are assaulting and fumbling the flowers/They call it easing the Spring."

9. In the context of the poem, the most capable and competent agent for bringing about positive change is

   a. the bee   b. the soldier
   c. the flower   d. the garden
   e. the gun

10. The poem is arranged and developed in all except one of the following ways:

   a. contrasting details   b. symbolism
   c. shifts in diction   d. imagistic details
   e. the fluctuating perspective of the speaker

Part II: Read the following poem carefully. Then, in a well-developed essay, show how the main idea of the poem is reinforced by all of the images.
(30 minutes)

Spring

Nothing is so beautiful as spring—
    When weeds, in wheels, shoot long and lovely and lush;
    Thrush's eggs look little low heavens, and thrush
Through the echoing timber does so rinse and wring

The ear, it strikes like lightnings to hear him sing;
    The glassy peartree leaves and blooms, they brush
    The descending blue; that is all in a rush
With richness; the racing lambs too have fair their fling.

What is all this juice and all this joy?
    A strain of the earth's sweet being in the beginning
In Eden garden.—Have, get, before it cloy,

Before it cloud, Christ, lord, and sour with sinning,
Innocent mind and Mayday in girl and boy,
    Most, O maid's child, thy choice and worthy the winning.

—Gerard Manley Hopkins

Part III
"What Are Patterns For?"

Introduction

Beyond the impact of individual words and phrases, poems are energized by arrangements that emerge from the ideas themselves or the manner in which they are presented. This sense of order may be evident on the sentence level; it may determine the stanzaic selection; it may control the pattern of the entire poem. Again, it is a question of "the best words in the best places."

The "best words," of course, influence the communicated meaning of any poem. Although many words are repeated in similar patterns, it is usually the variation, the fresh and original combination, that attracts our attention. Sustained word choices result also in the diction, the tone, and ultimately the theme of the poem.

Likewise, larger arrangements (in lines, sentences, and stanzas) help to shape the emotion and the logic of any communicated message.

Words that are chosen and arranged for their sound qualities not only have isolated effects, but also can help establish a mood, a tone, and a sense or order when patterned in various ways throughout the poem.

In a brief and beautiful lyric, Robert Herrick says it all:

Delight in Disorder

A sweet disorder in the dress
Kindles in clothes a wantonness.
A lawn about the shoulders thrown
Into a fine distraction;
An erring lace, which here and there
Enthralls the crimson stomacher;
A cuff neglectful, and thereby
Ribbons to flow confusedly;
A winning wave, deserving note,
In the tempestuous petticoat;
A careless shoestring, in whose tie
I see a wild civility;
Do more bewitch me than when art
Is too precise in every part.

The speaker is captivated by a "sweet disorder" which is paradoxically almost studied or planned. He imposes a wide variety of interpretations on this "ordered disorder." What, in effect, the poem suggests is that the best "art" does not readily reveal its pattern or organizing principles. It *seems* to happen by accident, not by artifice.

Lesson 19

"The Origin of All Poems": Repetition and Variation

Objectives

- To examine the role of repetition and variation in the poetic process
- To explore the impact of "order" on the communication of a "felt experience"

Notes to the Teacher

Walt Whitman, perhaps more than most poets, attempted to communicate a sense of himself through his poetry. Early in "Song of Myself" he tells his readers:

Stop this day and night with me and you
shall possess the origin of all poems
You shall possess the good of the earth and
sun, (There are millions of suns left,)
You shall no longer take things at second or
third hand, nor look through the eyes of
the dead, nor feed on the spectres in
books,
You shall not look through my eyes either,
nor take things from me,
You shall listen to all sides and filter them
from your self.

As this passage reveals, poems are from "all sides" and from within "your self." Whitman, of course, was talking about the process whereby he and each poet (and all of us are potential poets) discover the origin of poems within self, others, and the world in all of its complexity, here or hereafter.

While he dwells on his subject, however, we may not be alert to his method of development and presentation. If we were to read the entire poem (over 1500 lines), which functions as a prologue to his one poem, the ambitious *Leaves of Grass*, we would soon detect a sameness, a pattern, a stylistic repetition that is associated with Whitman.

In an essay on Whitman, Ezra Pound observed:

It is a great thing, reading a man, to know, not "His tricks are not as yet my tricks, but I can easily make them mine" but "His message is my message. We will see that men hear it."

Very few poets want to use the "tricks" of another poet. Stylistic imitation results in formulation, a loss of originality. As Pound points out, it is the message which survives and is found again and again in a new form of expression or a variation on an old one.

The brief excerpts from "Song of Myself" that accompany this lesson provide students with an opportunity to focus on the way feelings and ideas can be shaped by various syntactical patterns.

Procedure

1. Distribute **Handout 35.** Read the first passage for the students. Have them discuss the questions which follow it.

   Suggested Responses:

   Passage 1
   1. *He implies that we are all one ("every atom") and that he will sing and celebrate for all of us.*
   2. *It will be a celebration of a universal "self," yet also of a single self ("My tongue . . ." who has "roots" in this soil, is "now thirty-seven years old in perfect health.") Also it will not reflect (nor reject) any "creeds or schools," but "for good or bad," will be spontaneous ("Nature without check with original energy").*

2. Have students read and discuss the rest of the handout.

   Suggested Responses:

   Passage 2
   self: "flag of my disposition"
   God-given: "handkerchief of the Lord"
   new life: "itself a child"
   variety of life: "a uniform hieroglyphic"

symbol of democracy: "I give them the same, I receive them the same."
death: "beautiful uncut hair of graves"

Passage 3

1. Whitman is unconventional in his emphasis. He does not reject God or organized religion; he asserts the importance of every individual finding God within himself and "in the faces of men and women." He claims that this is the only way we can see and thus "understand" God. Knowledge and faith must be a concrete experience.

2. The emphasis is on balance, proportion and equality: body/soul; self/God; working man/hero; soul/universe; others/God. As a result, the emotions of the speaker are likewise balanced. If people are overwhelmed by God or the universe, how can they "stand cool and composed before a million universes" knowing that ". . . there is no object so soft but it makes a hub for the wheel'd universe." The tone is one of serenity.

Whitman's Style

1. Although answers will vary, students should note some of the following:
   The use of the first person speaker is very personal and directed to the reader as a participant in the poem.
   The poem as poem is foregrounded, a conscious activity on the part of the speaker.
   The images are very physical, even though they are usually in a universal context, striving to be representative of everyone and everything.

There is a complete absence of regular rhyme and meter; rhythm is achieved by a natural cadence which is usually achieved by a careful balancing of phrases and a repetition of grammatical patterns (i.e., free verse).
There is a very controlled use of figurative language. When employed, the details are usually physical things. The philosophical level of the poem is based on material aspects of reality even when metaphysically developed, e.g., the grass "is itself a child, the produced babe of the vegetation."
The diction is often expressive of the language and concerns of the common man ("I loaf": "I guess" the grass grows "among black folks as among white": and "no trade or employment but the young man following it may become a hero"). However, Whitman occasionally aspires to be "elegant" ("Wheresoe'er," "Be not," "to cease not"), lapsing into the poetic diction that dominated his age and those before it.

2. Pattern is achieved by the use of balance, parallelism, and inversion.

3. Answers will vary but should include some of the following points:
   Whitman is concerned with topics which we consider a reflection of the modern temper: self-awareness, physicality, spontaneity, unorthodox religious views.
   Whitman's style is much more personal than that of the earlier poets, avoiding the conventional characteristics of the poetry which preceded him, e.g., meter, rhyme, "ornate" diction.

"The Origin of All Poems"

Directions: Read the following excerpts from Walt Whitman's long poem, "Song of Myself," and answer the questions which follow each excerpt.

Passage 1:

> I celebrate myself, and sing myself,
> And what I assume you shall assume,
> For every atom belonging to me as good belongs to you.
>
> I loaf and invite my soul,
> I lean and loaf at my ease observing a spear of summer grass.
>
> My tongue, every atom of my blood, form'd from this soil, this air,
> Born here of parents born here from parents the same, and their parents
>   the same,
> I, now thirty-seven years old in perfect health begin,
> Hoping to cease not till death.
> Creeds and schools in abeyance,   10
> Retiring back a while sufficed at what they are, but never forgotten,
> I harbor for good or bad, I permit to speak at every hazard,
> Nature without check with original energy.

1. What is the basis for the speaker stating: ". . . what I assume you shall assume"?

2. What does the speaker indicate as characteristic of himself and his song?

Passage 2:

>A child said "What is the grass?" fetching it to me with full hands;
>How could I answer the child? I do not know what it is any more than he.
>I guess it must be the flag of my disposition, out of hopeful green
>>stuff woven.
>
>Or I guess it is the handkerchief of the Lord,
>A scented gift and remembrancer designedly dropt,
>Bearing the owner's name someway in the corners, that we may see and
>>remark, and say *Whose*?
>
>Or I guess the grass is itself a child, the produced babe of the
>>vegetation.
>
>Or I guess it is a uniform hieroglyphic,
>And it means, Sprouting alike in broad zones and narrow zones,
>Growing among black folks as among white,
>Kanuck, Tuckahoe, Congressman, Cuff, I give them the same, I receive
>>them the same.
>
>And now it seems to me the beautiful uncut hair of graves.

What is the grass? How does the speaker categorize its meanings?

Passage 3:

>I have said that the soul is not more than the body,
>And I have said that the body is not more than the soul,
>And nothing, not God, is greater to one than one's self is,
>And whoever walks a furlong without sympathy walks to his own
>>funeral drest in his shroud,
>And I or you pocketless of a dime may purchase the pick of the earth,
>And to glance with an eye or show a bean in its pod confounds the
>>learning of all times,
>And there is no trade or employment but the young man following it
>>may become a hero,

And there is no object so soft but it makes a hub for the wheel'd
    universe.
And I say to any man or woman, Let your soul stand cool and
    composed before a million universes.

And I say to mankind, Be not curious about God,
For I who am curious about each am not curious about God,
(No array of terms can say how much I am at peace about God and
    about death.)

I hear and behold God in every object, yet understand God not in
    the least,
Nor do I understand who there can be more wonderful than myself.

Why should I wish to see God better than this day?
I see something of God each hour of the twenty-four, and each
    moment then,
In the faces of men and women I see God, and in my own face in the glass,
I find letters from God dropt in the street, and every one is sign'd
    by God's name,
And I leave them where they are, for I know that wheresoe'er I go,
Others will punctually come for ever and ever.

1. Is the speaker egotistical when he says that ". . . nothing, not God, is greater to one than one's
    self is" or that he does not "understand who there can be more wonderful than myself"?

2. How has the speaker given shape to his emotions in this passage?

Whitman's Style:

1. How do the selections from "Song of Myself" differ from the following poems in point of view, diction, imagery, and other elements of style?

   a. "Hope" by George Herbert (**Handout 30**)

   b. "Ode on a Grecian Urn" by John Keats (**Handout 12**)

   c. "A Lecture on the Shadow" by John Donne (**Handout 20**)

2. How does Whitman impose "patterns" on his "song"?

3. Whitman has been called the "Father of Modern Poetry" even though he wrote in the nineteenth century. Donne, Herbert, and Keats all wrote prior to Whitman. Frost, Stevens, and Reed wrote after Whitman by almost a half century. Based on this information, can you come to any conclusions about why Whitman would be considered "modern"?

Lesson 20
Order in Disorder

Objective

- To examine the impact of syntax on the effect produced by a poem

Notes to the Teacher

Much attention is often paid to the way images, figures, symbols, and diction contribute to the impact of a poem. Syntax also contributes to the emotional life of a poem. The way words are arranged in sentences or stanzas often reflects the sense of order and the anticipated effect which the poem will produce. The way in which syntax produces these effects and the effects themselves are important. In themselves, the "tricks" of syntax are nothing more than grammatical and rhetorical techniques. In the context of art, they can become an organic aspect of any poem.

Procedure

1. Distribute **Handout 36.** Some of this may be used as a classroom activity with the entire group or be divided and completed in small groups. You may consider expanding the lesson by:
   a. examining the syntax of one or more poems
   b. asking students to add their own examples for each category

2. After students have completed **Handout 36,** conduct a discussion based on their explanations for each example.

   Suggested Responses:
   1. *The ungrammatical aspects highlight the conversational and unpretentious style of the speaker.*
   2. *The almost mechanical, routine activity is repeatedly referred to throughout the poem and provides a juxtaposed irony to the "naming of parts" of nature.*

3. a. *The variety in sentence length results in various impressions. The opening lines constitute a "chant," a personal hymn. The latter lines are more of a declamation.*
   b. *The staccatto effect of these stark lines underscores, avoiding all sentimentality, the human element of what is perceived as a symbolic, quasi-heroic act.*
4. *The coordination emphasizes the speaker's equation of friendship and pain and his desire to be isolated (like a rock or an island).*
5. *This is a dramatic emphasis on the fact that life goes on for the living, understated in the most unemotional terms. The impact results in a redirection from a potentially maudlin situation to a philosophical, rationalized outlook.*
6. *The questions intensify the emotional probing which the speaker engages in, generating new considerations.*
7. *The entire poem is one sentence—and a sonnet—which builds to a generalized resolution. This also provides an example of parallel structure.*
8. *The parallel ideas (with some correlations in grammatical construction) result in balance and clarity. In just these three lines the speaker identifies himself, his motives, and his relationship with his addressee.*
9. *The contrast results from the opposition in meaning between "art" and "chance" and the matter of degree suggested between basic movement and dance.*

Name _____

Date _____

Order in Disorder

Directions: The following syntactical considerations are defined and illustrated with examples from various poems, many from previous handouts. After each ex-
ample, state consisely the impact which each of these rhetorical arrangements has on the communicated feeling or idea of the poem.

1. Run-on Sentence: two sentences expressed as one
    and
   Fragment: an incomplete sentence

   Example: "The taking of our lives—lives of a good shoemaker and a
              poor fishpeddler—
            all! That last moment belongs to us—
            that agony is our triumph."

                                             ("Last Speech to the Court"
                                             —Bartolomeo Vanzetti, **Handout 4**)

2. Repetition: By echoing words, clauses, sentences, and even entire stanzas (e.g., a
   chorus), a poet can emphasize an important idea or emotion.

   Example: "Today we have naming of parts."

                                   ("Naming of Parts" —Henry Reed, **Handout 34**)

3. **Sentence Length:** The grammatical complexity (or simplicity) of a sentence can produce varied effects.

    a. Variety: Example:

        See "Song of Myself" —Walt Whitman (**Handout 35,** Passage 1)

    b. Conciseness: Example:

        "He burned. He suffered.
        He died."

                ("Norman Morrison" —Adrian Mitchel, **Handout 1**)

4. **Coordination:** an expression of equal relationship of two ideas in one sentence.

    Example: "I have no need of friendship;
              friendship causes pain."

                ("I Am a Rock" —Paul Simon, **Handout 15**)

5. Subordination: the expression of a less important idea in conjunction with a more important one.

   Example: "...And they, since they
              Were not the one dead, turned to their affairs."

                                   ("Out, Out—" —Robert Frost, **Handout 2**)

6. Rhetorical Question: an obvious question which does not call for a stated reply.

   Example: "Did you think the son would shine?...
              What was there to forgive?..."

                                   ("Daddy" —Patrick Middleton, **Handout 6**)

7. Periodic Sentence: an arrangement of detail, usually in a series of introductory subordinate clauses, that leads to a climactic final statement.

   Example: "when serpents bargain for the right to squirm"

                                   (entire poem—E. E. Cummings **Handout 30**)

8. Parallelism: structuring sentence elements (coordinated ideas, correlated construc-
        tions, compared and contrasted ideas) in similarly expressed ways.

    Example: "I celebrate myself, and sing myself,
                And what I assume you shall assume.
                For every atom belonging to me as good belongs to you."

                            ("Song of Myself" —Walt Whitman, **Handout 35**)

9. Antithesis: a contrast in the position of words and/or their meaning.

    Example: "True ease in writing comes from art, not chance,
                As those move easiest who have learned to dance."

                            ("Sound and Sense" —Alexander Pope, **Handout 14**)

Lesson 21
The Shape of a Poem

Objective

- To categorize, define, and examine the various structural and formal conventions which influence the shape of poetic discourse

Notes to the Teacher

A poet chooses words, arranges them into sentences or units of poetic insight, and combines sentences into larger units of meaning (e.g., stanzas) in order to give structure and form to an imagined experience. This fictive process results in what we identify as "the poem." Other predetermined factors, however, may influence the mode of this message. The history of poetic expression has provided many empty poetry containers ready to be filled.

The poem may focus on a description of the imagined experience, resulting, for example, in an adoption of the conventions of concrete, haiku, or imagistic poetry. If the significance of the specific details is emphasized and rationalized, symbolic poetry may result. The poem may be based on what Wordsworth called "the spontaneous overflow of powerful feeling," and the conventions of the lyric (ode, elegy, pastoral, sonnet, or pure lyric) may be employed. A rational emphasis may be on narration, resulting in soliloquy, dramatic monologue or dialogue, ballad, or epic.

Some poems are also organized by external factors, usually sound structure. Certain patterns of meter and rhyme may be imposed on a poem. The English (Shakespearean) sonnet, for example, is typically written in iambic pentameter with a predetermined rhyme scheme (abab cdcd efef gg). Villanelle, triolet, rondel, terza rima, blank verse, ballad, quatrains, rhyme royal, and heroic couplets are just a few of the many fixed forms which a poet can employ in an effort to achieve poetic unity.

The shape of a poem can be generated by the subject (e.g., elegy) or be imposed by the imitation of a preexisting form (e.g., sonnet). It is one way that a poet can give order and logic to what is primarily a felt experience and expression. No poet and or poem totally abandons the conventions of poetic discourse. Some poets may (thankfully) experiment with ways of writing, but poetic discourse builds on the resources of language which require a certain degree of adherence in order to make any communication possible. Each poem is a repetition and variation on preexisting structures. At the same time that a poem is an empty container waiting to be filled, it is also an ocean waiting for a "well wrought urn."

Procedure

1. Distribute **Handout 37**. Review the definitions in the context of the background provided above. Students should come to an understanding of the concept of literary conventions as a major influence on the communication process in poetry. Poems, like all art forms, are artifacts of the ages which produced them, reflecting the vision and values, the language and learning of their cultural climates.

2. Give students in small groups about twenty minutes to categorize titles of poems from all of their handouts. Warn them that poems can be cross-referenced.

3. Discuss the categories with the students.

   Suggested Responses:
   Some categories are not represented on handouts which the students have used so far. They should be aware of this based on definitions and examples.
   Imagistic/Descriptive Development
   1. *Concrete Poem: no previous examples*
   2. *Haiku: no previous examples*
   3. *Imagistic Treatment of Subject: "Player Piano"* (**Handout 14**); *"Old Houses"* (**Handout 28**); *"The Moon"* (**Handout 28**)
   4. *Symbolic Treatment of Subject: "The Wayfarer"* (**Handout 33**); *"Many*

Workmen" (**Handout 33**); *"Hope"* (**Handout 32**); *"Hope Is the Thing with Feathers"* (**Handout 32**); *"The Emperor of Ice Cream"* (**Handout 30**); *"No Images"* (**Handout 28**)

Lyrical Development

1. *Ode: "Ode to Ben Jonson"* (**Handout 13**); *"Ode on a Grecian Urn"* (**Handout 12**)
2. *Elegy: "On the Late Massacre in Piedmont"* (**Handout 24**); *"Out, Out—"* (**Handout 2**); *"Daddy"* (**Handout 7**); *"Of Late"* (**Handout 1**); *"Norman Morrison"* —Ferguson (**Handout 1**); *"Norman Morrison"—Mitchell* (**Handout 1**)
3. *Sonnet: "Spring"* (**Handout 34**); *"when serpents bargain for the right to squirm"* (**Handout 30**); *"On the Late Massacre in Piedmont"* (**Handout 24**);
4. *Lyrical Treatment of Subject: "Naming of Parts"* (**Handout 34**); *"Song of Myself"* (**Handout 35**); *"I Know I'm Not Sufficiently Obscure"* (**Handout 26**); *"The Promised Land"* (**Handout 15**); *"I Am a Rock"* (**Handout 15**); *"Preface to a Poetry Reading"* (**Handout 14**); *"Nobody Comes"* (**Handout 10**); *"Happy Father's Day"* (**Handout 6**); *"Daddy"* (**Handout 6**); *"Last Speech to the Court"* (**Handout 4**); *"Justice Denied in Massachusetts"* (**Handout 4**)

5. *Meditative Treatment of Subject: "The World"* (**Handout 33**); *"Spring"* (**Handout 34**); *"Ode on a Grecian Urn"* (**Handout 12**)
6. *Logical Treatment of Subject: "when serpents bargain for the right to squirm"* (**Handout 30**); *"Very Like a Whale"* (**Handout 29**)

Narrative Development

1. *Soliloquy: no examples*
2. *Dramatic Monologue: "A Lecture on the Shadow"* (**Handout 20**) *is an example of a dramatic monologue, but the treatment is lyrical rather than narrative.*
3. *Dramatic Dialogue: This mode is not very common in poetry and when it is employed, it is usually developed in ballads (e.g., "Lord Randall") or in a lyrical "debate."*
4. *Third Person Speaker/Objective: "Out, Out—"* (**Handout 2**); *all three poems about Norman Morrison* (**Handout 1**) *have narrative qualities, but the basic treatment is lyrical (elegaic).*

4. Assign students a structural technique from **Handout 38**. Ask them to report (in either oral or written form) to the class on the impact of this structural technique on the development of a specific poem. They may select a listed poem or choose their own.

The Shape of a Poem

Directions: Listed below are definitions of various types of poems which have influenced the shaping of poetry in the last five hundred years or more. Poets have often consciously imitated these structural and formal conventions. You have already encountered many of these in your study of poetry. Work according to directions provided by your teacher and provide examples for each definition. Use only **Handout 1-36.** Examples are provided for categories for which there are no examples. Be prepared to discuss your grouping with the class.

Imagistic/Descriptive Development

1. Concrete/Descriptive Development: an arrangement of words to reflect the meaning of a poem

    Example:

2. Haiku: a single image from nature; 17 syllables in 3 lines (5-7-5)

    Example: Three loveliest things—
    Moonlight, cherry bloom, I go
    Seeking silent snow.

3. Imagistic Treatment of Subject: Emphasis on concrete, specific detail; appeal to the senses

    Example:

4. Symbolic Treatment of Subject: things stand for abstractions

    Example:

Lyrical Development

1. Ode: a long formal, serious lyric written in a complex form
   Example:

2. Elegy: a lament, usually for the death of a particular person
   Example:

3. Sonnet: a fourteen-line lyric which is usually divided into an octave and sestet (Italian/ Petrachan) or three quatrains and a couplet (English/Shakespearean); a specific meter/rhyme is usually employed; an idea or emotion is usually developed.
   Example:

4. Lyrical Treatment of Subject: an emphasis on emotional and subjective responses
   Example:

5. Meditative Treatment of Subject: the subject is contemplated and responded to in somewhat emotional terms.
   Example:

6. Logical Treatment of Subject: the subject is contemplated and responded to in somewhat logical/rational terms.
   Example:

Narrative Development

1. Soliloquy: one speaker thinks out loud and tells a story

   Example: The lines alluded to in Robert Frost's poem, "Out, Out—," are from a solilo-
   quy in Shakespeare's *Macbeth*:
   > "Out, out brief candle!
   > Life's but a walking shadow."

2. Dramatic Monologue: a speaker with an implied listener

   Example:

3. Dramatic Dialogue: an exchange between two speakers

   Example: The passage from Shakespeare's *Hamlet* (**Handout 28**) is dramatic dialogue but not narrative *per se*. This mode is not common in poetry and
   when it is employed it is usually in ballads or debates.

4. Third Person Speaker/Objective: The narrator is distanced from the narrative as an
   observer of the action.

   Example:

Name _____

Date _____

Empty Containers: Well Wrought Urns

Directions: You will report on how the external structure of a poem, the way it conforms to certain predetermined guidelines, influences the shape and impact of its message. The poems listed under each heading are possible choices. You also have the option of choosing your own example.

1. Villanelle: consists of five tercets and one quatrain; the first and third lines of the first tercet are alternately repeated as final lines of the tercets which follow and are used together as a couplet in the quatrain

   Examples: "Do Not Go Gentle into That Good Night" —Dylan Thomas
   "The Waking" —Theodore Roethke
   "Missing Dates" —William Empson

2. Terza Rima: iambic pentameter lines rhyming aba, bcb, cdc, etc.

   Examples: "Ode to the West Wind" —Percey Bysshe Shelley
   "Acquainted with the Night" —Robert Frost

3. Blank Verse: unrhymed iambic pentameter

   Examples: "Thanatopsis" —William Cullen Bryant
   "Sunday Morning" —Wallace Stevens
   "The Second Coming" —William Butler Yeats
   "Ulysses" —Alfred, Lord Tennyson

4. Ballad Quatrains: alternating tetrameter and trimeter lines usually rhyming abab

   Examples: "Strange Fits of Passion Have I Known" —William Wordsworth
   "Proud Maisie" —Sir Walter Scott
   "A Slumber Did My Spirit Steal" —William Wordsworth
   "Because I Could Not Stop for Death" —Emily Dickinson

5. Rhyme Royal: seven iambic pentameter lines rhyming ababbcc

   Example: "They Flee from Me" —Sir Thomas Wyatt

6. Heroic Couplet: a rhyming pentameter couplet which incorporates a complete thought

   Examples: "An Essay on Criticism" —Alexander Pope
   "To Heaven" —Ben Jonson
   "Good Friday, 1613, Riding Westward" —John Donne

Lesson 22
Withered Sledge on the Fields of Eden: Tonal Structure

Objective

• To identify and explore the impact of tonal structure

Notes to the Teacher

When all of the parts of a poem are unified, tonal structure clarifies what is stated. Tonality defines the attitude of the speaker toward the subject and the listener. By implication, the attitude of the poet toward the subject of the poem, at least imaginatively, is inherent in the tone of the poem.

Tone can be elusive and complex. The spoken word can rather easily communicate a variety of tones by a mere inflection of the speaker's voice. The written word, however, must incorporate tone into a given context by a careful orchestration of well chosen words which have imagistic and connotative qualities appropriate to the poet's purpose. The rhythm, or potential aural impact of the discourse, is also an important factor in establishing tone.

Procedure

1. Distribute and review **Handout 39.** Clarify parts of the handout in response to students' questions. Indicate that there is no specific formula for determining tone. Tone is organic to each poem and should be assessed after careful reading and consideration of various other elements. A misreading of the poem results when the tone is not accurately detected.

2. Distribute **Handout 40.** Ask students, working in small groups, to formulate a statement about the tone of each poem and be prepared to describe how the tone of each is communicated.

Suggested Responses:

"In Westminster Abbey"
The poem is a dramatic monologue in the form of a prayer. The content of the prayer ironically reveals the prejudice and vanity of the self-centered speaker. Only a reader who shares these views would read the poem and remain insensitive to its satiric tone. With God on her side and the side of white, middle-class British subjects, the speaker has an idea of a God who is at her convenience, protecting her stocks, her country and her provincialism.

"La Belle Dame sans Merci"
Much of the imagery and diction of the poem is associated with the world of romance: the "knight-at-arms" and his lady, the "pacing steed," the "faery's song." However, the setting and narrative development also suggest the Gothic romance; a wasteland where "no birds sing" and the "sledge has withered," hints of bewitchment, a death-dream, etc. The tone is earnest. The treatment of the subject is emotionally controlled, leaving it up to the reader to respond to the plight of the knight and the dark side of the world of romance.

3. Students may benefit from an analysis of the tones of various previously studied poems.

A Guide to Tonal Analysis

Tone is the attitude and feeling that an author takes toward the subject. Tone is achieved by a variety of elements within the discourse: diction, imagery, sound structures.

Directions: The following questions will help you to determine the tone of almost any poem that you read. Review them with your teacher and apply them to your interpretation of the tones of the two poems on **Handout 40.**

Basic Questions

1. Is the speaker sincere or insincere in the treatment of the subject?

2. Is the attitude of the speaker intellectual or emotional or a combination of both?

3. What does the attitude tell us about the speaker's point of view, prejudices, values, etc.?

4. Is there a shift in tone as the discourse develops?

Tonal Analysis

1. If you detect:

    extreme sincerity
    idealized outlooks
    categorical virtues/vices and heroes/villains
    excessive optimism

    then the tone may be romantic.

2. If you detect:

    straightforwardness
    profound awareness of mortality
    a sense of loss of perfection/goodness
    an awareness of sin and evil
    a fall from greatness

    then the tone may be tragic.

3. If you detect:

    a sense of disillusionment

    a distrust of all appearances

    a mocking, flippant, irreverent, sarcastic, pessimistic or even contemptuous or cynical outlook

        then the tone may be satiric or ironic.

4. If you detect:

    a moderated optimism

    a realistic belief in perfectability

    a hope for improvement

        then the tone may be comedic.

Communication through Tone

In Westminster Abbey

Let me take this other glove off
   As the *vox humana* swells,
And the beauteous fields of Eden
   Bask beneath the Abbey bells.
Here, where England's statesmen lie,
Listen to a lady's cry.

Gracious Lord, oh bomb the Germans.
   Spare their women for Thy Sake,
And if that is not too easy
   We will pardon Thy Mistake.
But, gracious Lord, whate'er shall be,
Don't let anyone bomb me.

Keep our Empire undismembered
   Guide our Forces by Thy Hand.
Gallant blacks from far Jamaica,
   Honduras and Togoland;
Protect them Lord in all their fights,
And, even more, protect the whites.

Think of what our Nation stands for,
   Books from Boots and country lanes,
Free speech, free passes, class distinction,
   Democracy and proper drains.
Lord, put beneath Thy special care
One-eighty-nine Cadogan Square.

Although dear Lord I am a sinner
   I have done no major crime
Now I'll come to Evening Service
   Whensoever I have time
So, Lord, reserve for me a crown
And do not let my shares go down.

I will labor for Thy Kingdom,
   Help our lads to win the war
Send white feathers to the cowards
   Join the Women's Army Corps

Then wash the Steps around Thy Throne
In the Eternal Safety Zone

Now I feel a little better,
   What a treat to hear Thy Word,
Where the bones of leading statesmen,
   Have so often been interr'd.
And now, dear Lord I cannot wait
Because I have a luncheon date.

—John Betjeman

La Belle Dame sans Merci

"O what can ail thee, knight-at-arms,
   Alone and palely loitering?
The sedge has withered from the lake,
   And no birds sing.

"O what can ail thee, knight-at-arms,
   So haggard and so woebegone?
The squirrel's granary is full,
   And the harvest's done.

"I see a lily on thy brow
   With anguish moist and fever-dew,
And on thy cheeks a fading rose
   Fast withereth, too."

"I met a lady in the meads,
   Full beautiful—a faery's child;
Her hair was long, her foot was light,
   And her eyes were wild.

"I made a garland for her head,
   And bracelets, too, and fragrant zone;
She looked at me as she did love,
   And made sweet moan.

"I set her on my pacing steed
   And nothing else saw all day long
For sidelong would she bend, and sing
   A faery's song.

"She found me roots of relish sweet,
   And honey wild and manna-dew
And sure in language strange she said,
   'I love thee true.'

"She took me to her elfin grot,
   And there she wept and sighed full sore;
And there I shut her wild, wild eyes
   With kisses four.

"And there she lulled me asleep,
 And there I dreamed—Ah! woe betide!
The latest dream I ever dreamed
 On the cold hill's side.

"I saw pale kings and princes, too,
 Pale warriors, death-pale were they all
They cried—'La belle dame sans merci
 Hath thee in thrall!'

"I saw their starved lips in the gloam
 With horrid warning gaped wide,
And I awoke and found me here
 On the cold hill's side.

"And this is why I sojourn here,
 Alone and palely loitering,
Though the sedge is withered from the lake,
 And no birds sing."

        —John Keats

Lesson 23

Beauty and Truth: Philosophical Patterns

Objectives

- To examine the structure of ideas in the total development of a poem
- To define theme and trace its development in specific poems

Notes to the Teacher

Every poem has a theme, a significant idea, a foundation on which to build. In some poetry the idea is well explored and developed; in other poetry it is just a slight element of cohesion. Note, for example, T. E. Hulme's slight, imagistic lyric:

> Old houses were scaffolding once
> and workmen whistling.

Here, the idea does not dominate the image; the image communicates the idea. It could be restated as:

> For every cause there is
> an effect.

This statement, however, ignores the elements of time ("Old...once"), process ("scaffolding" becomes "old houses"), and contrast (inanimate "old houses" now vs. animate "workmen whistling" then). It is evident that a poem is not easily reduced to a paraphrase or an abstraction. Because of the poem's compression, a paraphrase usually entails more words and explanations. If this is true of these two lines, how much more difficult it is with longer, more intricately developed poems such as John Donne's "A Lecture Upon the Shadow" or John Keats' "Ode on a Grecian Urn."

A statement of theme must reflect all that the poem is about, not just part of it; it must take into account the various elements—imagery, figures, symbols, tone—which contribute to the poem's development. Consequently, it must abstract from all of the "appearances" of the poem, even its supposed subject, in order to universalize the real "message" of the poem.

In some poems, such as Emily Dickinson's "I Died for Beauty," the abstraction is close to the surface. The difficulty often results in justifying the specifics. In other poems, the theme is embedded in organic development. In Keats' "Ode on a Grecian Urn" there may be a tendency to read the final lines as a definitive statement of theme for the entire poem:

> 'Beauty is truth, truth Beauty'—that is all
> Ye know on earth, and all ye need to know.

To do so, however, would ignore very important ideas and qualifications which the entire text of the poem poses. The thematic structure of a poem incorporates the philosophy, the world view of that poem. Theme cannot be stated as a half-truth; it must be total.

Procedure

1. Distribute **Handout 41.** Discuss the concept of theme as outlined above. Emphasize the fact that a statement of theme must take into account all of the major elements of the poem and that it must be abstract, not reflecting specific details of the poem. Indicate that a theme is not confined to one poem but can be repeated in others. Indicate that the subject of the poem is not the theme. Both Dickinson's "I Died for Beauty" and Keats' "Ode on a Grecian Urn" deal with the subject of beauty and truth, but in very different ways. Of course there is very little critical consensus on the theme of many poems. Stress with students the need to justify their conclusions based on their understanding of the texts.

Possible Reponses:

Theme: The Supremacy of Art over Life

Life is characterized by mortality and impermanence. It is transitory. The

Grecian Urn, paradoxically, is a "still un-ravish'd bride of quietness" yet a "sylvan historian" or "cold pastoral" that communicates a message to mankind: "Beauty is truth, truth beauty." But art's message is only meaningful to one who looks at life in transcendental terms along the lines illustrated in the poem. In the real world we cannot hear "ditties of no tone" or appreciate an unacquired kiss. Their beauty, and consequently their truth, escape us. But in the world of the imagination, the beauty of unheard melodies and idealized love has a "truth" of its own. Therefore, in this world, if we are willing to acknowledge the supremacy of artistic expression and experience, all we need to know is that: "Beauty is truth, truth beauty."

Theme: Beauty and Truth after Death Are One

The dialogue between two "martyrs" who have died for beauty and truth reveals a kinship: "We brethern, are." In a world of appearances, however, this affinity is not evident. In death, it is too late.

Identity and communication are no longer possible:

> . . . the moss had reached our lips—
> and covered up—our names—

Nature prevails as it obscures all traces of life. Eventually, it is immortality which prevails.

2. Distribute **Handout 42.** Students may complete this in small groups or as homework. Use it as the basis of a follow-up discussion.

Suggested Responses:
1. *Eternity is only for the faithful.*
2. *The circumstances of life sometimes interfere with self-realization.*
3. *The greatest love is open and without deceit.*
4. *Isolation and loneliness are accentuated by the activity of others.*
5. *Life is meaningless in a world without justice.*
6. *The world of nature is more powerful than the world of routine and violence.*

Name _____

Date _____

Philosophical Considerations

Directions: Compare the treatments of beauty and truth in the following poem and in Keats' "Ode on a Grecian Urn" (**Handout 12**). Attempt to arrive at a statement of theme for each poem.

I Died for Beauty

I died for Beauty—but was scarce
Adjusted in the Tomb
When One who died for Truth, was lain
In an adjoining Room—

He questioned softly "Why I failed"?
"For Beauty," I replied—
"And I—for Truth—Themselves are One—
We Bretheren, are," He said—

And so, as Kinsmen, met a Night—
We talked between the Rooms—
Until the Moss had reached our lips—
And covered up—our names—

—Emily Dickinson

Theme:

    "Ode on a Grecian Urn":

    "I Died for Beauty":

Name _____

Date _____

Themes

Directions: State in one sentence the themes of the following poems.

1. "The World" (**Handout 33**)

2. "No Images" (**Handout 28**)

3. "A Lecture Upon the Shadow" (**Handout 20**)

4. "Nobody Comes" (**Handout 10**)

5. "Justice Denied in Massachusetts (**Handout 4**)

6. "Naming of Parts" (**Handout 34**)

Lesson 24

"In Darkness I Must Dwell": The Tragic Pattern

Objectives

- To relate the philosophy of poetry to the realities of life
- To examine and demonstrate the concept of genre to explain the dimensions of the tragic vision.

Notes to the Teacher

A poem's patterns achieve unity and coherence through varied techniques. Additional patterns embodied in poetry reflect real life patterns. Just as we see patterns in nature (cycles of the day and the seasons) which reflect what we see in ourselves (youth, maturity, old age, and death), our imagination extends this awareness into literature. Consequently, literary genres incorporate specific world views.

The basic literary genres are patterns that our imagination imposes upon experience and literary form. Our experience of ourselves and nature reveals:

1. youth, innocence and perfection, a world imaged in pastoral and utopian literature;
2. knowledge and loss of innocence, a world imaged in tragic literature;
3. disillusionment and contradictions, a world imaged in ironic and satirical literature;
4. hope, optimism, and rebirth, a world imaged in comedic literature.

Genre is also an influence on tonal structure and style (e.g., pastoral elegy, mock epic, tragic ballad).

These ideas form the basis of archetypal analysis. According to Jung, all literary expression is a statement derived from communal consciousness. What is expressed is universal because it reflects the shared experiences of human nature at any time and in any place. In this way, the similarities of different literary characters, themes, rituals, images, and stories can be explained. It is not a question of influence or imitation, but a shared imaginative perspective based on common experiences that transcend time and place.

We find romance, tragedy, satire, and comedy in various works of literature. In some, one pattern dominates; in others, it is a matter of degree. In Keats' "La Belle Dame sans Merci" (**Handout 40**), the romantic vision is evident but the tragic is inevitable. The young knight is bewitched and in the thrall of his lady. Innocence is corrupted. Even in Eden a serpent "bargains for the right to squirm." "In Westminster Abbey" (**Handout 40**) encompasses a disillusioned perspective of human nature. All ideals and hopes for human perfectability are reversed; human nature is self-centered and has adopted a practical approach to religion. The double perspective of a tragic vision is evident in the poems in this lesson: Amy Lowell's "Patterns" and a song lyric with the same title by Simon and Garfunkel. In each, the speaker considers the impact of patterns on the way we live. Like Archibald MacLeish's *J.B.*, a thinly disguised scriptural Job, both of the speakers in these poems in effect cry out:

> If God is God, He is not good.
> If God is good, He is not God, . .

This is the dilemma that tragedy highlights, the age old question of good and evil. How can they coexist in a world created and governed by a good and just God? Keats (in "Ode on a Grecian Urn") and Dickinson (in "I Died for Beauty") found an answer in transcendence, a hope that the best will prevail either here or hereafter. Poets who are immersed in the tragic, however, often attempt to ask and answer the question again and again in completely human terms. In the *Poetics* Aristotle pinpointed *hubris* (human pride in defiance of the gods) and the consequent *hamartia* (error in judgment) as the source of tragedy.

Procedure

1. Explain and elaborate upon archetypal theory as outlined in the notes above. Ask students to cite examples of each genre

155

based on their reading of various poems. Be flexible, emphasizing the fact that elements are often combined. Challenge students to detect dominant archetypal patterns.

2. Distribute **Handout 43.** If possible, play recorded versions of both poems. ("Patterns" by Simon and Garfunkel is in the album entitled *Parsley, Sage, Rosemary, and Thyme.*)
   Allow students to give direction to the discussion. With the Lowell poem it may be necessary to provide some background on the time period (eighteenth century) suggested by the clothing (brocade, powdered hair, stays) and formal garden.

3. Before the discussion becomes too scattered, you may advise students to focus attention on five key questions on the handout. Ask students to make comparisons and decide if the poems are statements of identical themes.

Suggested Responses:

Answers should cover some of the following points.

"Patterns" by Amy Lowell

The speaker at first seems to identify with them ("I too am a rare/Pattern") in her way of dress and her environment ("patterned garden"), but in her imagination she stages a rebellion ("What is summer in a fine brocaded gown?"). The acceptance of pattern is still reflected in her conventional behavior ("See that the messenger takes some refreshment") even as she learns of the death of her husband-to-be. There is no emotional outburst, only a patterned walk "Up and down" the garden path. In the final lines she notes the relationship of her patterns to those in nature ("The squills and daffo-

dils/Will give place to pillared roses, and to asters, and to snow"), but still sees herself as conforming to a pattern ("I shall go/Up and down./In my gown."). She now sees "patterns" as a defense ("my body will be guarded from embrace") even though she is still baffled by the larger patterns (e.g., war) which have overshadowed her own personal patterns of existence. The rebellion of the speaker, however, seems to be more an outlet for grief than an expression of despair. She goes through the motions, keeping up appearances from the outset.

"Patterns" by Simon and Garfunkel

The speaker sees the patterns in nature as symbolic of the pattern of his own existence. Images of nature are autumnal; day is turning into night. The artificial "light from the street lamp" penetrates the darkness of his isolation ("narrow little room") but it does not provide enlightenment, only a puzzle (". . . the puzzle that is me"). He accepts his fate ("There are patterns I must follow . . . '), but is "like a rat in a maze." The speaker is ambivalent in his view of fate. Stanza three suggests that fate must be accepted as natural, like breathing and dying. Yet in the final stanza there is an emphasis on the control that fate exerts by way of factors such as age and race.

Both poems regard fate as overwhelming. It controls and manipulates our lives. The speaker in Lowell's poem questions its meaning and challenges its authority. In Simon and Garfunkel's lyrics, the speaker seems resigned to live a life that "can scarcely be controlled."

"What Are Patterns For?"

Directions: Read the following two poems and answer the questions which follow. Discuss the tragic vision, which each poem reflects in a different way.

Patterns

I walk down the garden-paths,
And all the daffodils
Are blowing, and the bright blue squills.
I walk down the patterned garden-paths
In my stiff, brocaded gown.   5
With my powdered hair and jewelled fan,
I too am a rare
Pattern. As I wander down
The garden-paths.
My dress is richly figured,   10
And the train
Makes a pink and silver stain
On the gravel, and the thrift
Of the borders.
Just a plate of current fashion,   15
Tripping by in high-heeled, ribboned shoes.
Not a softness anywhere about me,
Only whale-bone and brocade.
And I sink on a seat in the shade
Of a lime-tree. For my passion   20
Wars against the stiff brocade.
The daffodils and squills
Flutter in the breeze
As they please.
And I weep;   25
For the lime-tree is in blossom
And one small flower had dropped upon my bosom.

And the plashing of waterdrops
In the marble fountain
Comes down the garden-paths.   30
The dripping never stops.
Underneath my stiffened gown
Is the softness of a woman bathing in a marble basin,
A basin in the midst of hedges grown
So thick, she cannot see her lover hiding,   35

But she guesses he is near,
And the sliding of the water
Seems the stroking of a dear
Hand upon her.
What is Summer in a fine brocaded gown!   40
I should like to see it lying in a heap upon the ground.
All the pink and silver crumpled up on the ground.

I would be the pink and silver as I ran along the paths,
And he would stumble after
Bewildered by my laughter.   45
I should see the sun flashing from his sword hilt and the
      buckles on his shoes.
I would choose
To lead him in a maze along the patterned paths,
A bright and laughing maze for my heavy-booted lover,
Till he caught me in the shade,   50
And the buttons of his waistcoat bruised my body as he
      clasped me,
Aching, melting, unafraid,
With the shadows of the leaves and the sundrops,
And the plopping of the waterdrops,
All about us in the open afternoon—   55
I am very like to swoon
With the weight of this brocade,
For the sun sifts through the shade.
Underneath the fallen blossom
In my bosom,   60
Is a letter I have hid.
It was brought to me this morning by a rider from the Duke.
"Madam, we regret to inform you that Lord Hartwell
Died in action Thursday se'nnight."
As I read it in the white, morning sunlight,   65
The letters squirmed like snakes.
"Any answer, Madam," said my footman.
"No," I told him.
"See that the messenger takes some refreshment.
No, no answer."   70
And I walked into the garden,
Up and down the patterned paths,
In my stiff, correct brocade.
The blue and yellow flowers stood up proudly in the sun,
Each one.   75
I stood upright too,
Held rigid to the pattern

By the stiffness of my gown.
Up and down I walked,
Up and down.   80

In a month he would have been my husband.
In a month, here, underneath this lime,
We would have broke the pattern;
He for me, and I for him,
He as Colonel, I as Lady,   85
On this shady seat.
He had a whim
That sunlight carried blessing.
And I answered, "It shall be as you have said."
Now he is dead.   90

In Summer and in Winter I shall walk
Up and down
The patterned garden-paths
In my stiff, brocaded gown.
The squills and daffodils   95
Will give place to pillared roses, and to asters, and to snow.
I shall go
Up and down,
In my gown.
Gorgeously arrayed,   100
Boned and stayed.
And the softness of my body will be guarded from embrace
By each button, hook, and lace.
For the man who should loose me is dead,
Fighting with the Duke in Flanders,
In a pattern called a war.
Christ! What are patterns for?

—Amy Lowell

Patterns

The night sets softly with the hush of falling leaves.
Casting shivering shadows on the houses through the trees.
And the light from the street lamp makes a pattern on my wall,
Like the pieces of a puzzle or a child's uneven scrawl.

Up a narrow flight of stairs in a narrow little room,
As I lie upon my bed in the early evening gloom,
Impaled on my wall my eyes can dimly see
The pattern of my life and the puzzle that is me.

From the moment of my birth to the instant of my death,
There are patterns I must follow just as I must breathe each breath.
Like a rat in a maze the path before me lies,
And the pattern never alters until the rat dies.

The pattern still remains on the wall where darkness fell,
And it's fitting that it should for in darkness I must dwell.
Like the color of my skin or the day that I grow old,
My life is made of patterns that can scarcely be controlled.

—Paul Simon

	Lowell	Simon & Garfunkel
1. What is the attitude of the speaker toward "patterns"?		
2. In the context of the poem, what do "patterns" symbolize?		
3. What images or figures of speech does the poet use to reinforce the symbolism?		
4. How does the poem reflect despair or hope in its tragic awareness?		
5. How do the poems differ in thematic development?		

Lesson 25
"After the First Death, There Is No Other": Comedic Resolution

Objective

- To explore the dimensions of the comedic vision

Notes to the Teacher

Just as students often confuse the pathetic with the genuinely tragic, so they often associate the comedic exclusively with humor and laughter. The common use of the word "comic" reinforces this connection. If laughter can be linked with the revitalization process, whereby human nature triumphantly rejoices in overcoming the obstacles offered by life, then the classical, more literary meaning of the word prevails.

Comedy is expressed in overcoming obstacles, escaping the maze, and celebrating achievement. This celebration very often is ritualized in some kind of "happy ever after" ending: a party, a wedding, a birth.

Procedure

1. A poem such as Dylan Thomas's "A Refusal to Mourn the Death, by Fire, of a Child in London" gives students some perspective. In form, it is a rare breed: a comedic, elegiac anti-elegy. Students readily agree that there is nothing "comic" in the popular sense about the subject of the poem. "How is it comedic?" they may ask. "Where is the party, the wedding, the birth?" Of course, that is not all that is likely troubling them. The syntactical experimentation and metaphoric density are often the basis for initial confusion. Distribute **Handout 44** and give them the opportunity to confront some of these issues.

2. Read the poem for the students (or use a recorded version) at least twice. Allow time for their ears to adjust to the varied rhythms. Their minds may be confused by the "jumbled meaning."

Consider the discussion questions with the students, or have them work together in small groups.

Suggested Responses:

The following points should be brought out in the discussion.

First Stanza: third person speaker

The "Darkness" is depicted as "fathering" all that is: mankind, bird, beast, flower. It "Tells with silence" of itself ("the last light breaking") during the "still hour" when the sea is calm ("in harness"). In other words, darkness is the agent which creates and communicates.

Second Stanza: first person speaker

The speaker says that he must "enter the water bead" ("round Zion") the "ear of corn" ("synagogue") and "pray" (with "the shadow of a sound") and weep and mourn ("sow my salt seed" or tears) in the "valley of sackcloth." The imagery is suggestive here of the "valley of the shadow of death" where the Psalmist does not fear because the Lord protects him. In other words, the speaker refuses to weep and mourn in traditional (i.e. ancient biblical) ways.

Third Stanza: first person speaker

The function of the run-on idea is to link the Old and New Testaments, with the New Testament promising resurrection. The speaker states that he will not "murder" or "blaspheme" the memory of the child with "a grave truth" (pun?) or an "elegy of innocence and youth." Murder, blasphemy, and "stations of the breath" are suggestive of the death of Christ, a salvific act intended to save mankind from eternal death.

Fourth Stanza: third person speaker

The "grave truths" are revealed: "London's daughter" is now "deep with the first dead," robed (like a grain that will grow again), nurtured by "her mother" (earth) who will nourish her (with "unmourning water") for resurrection ("after the first death, there is no other"). Just as darkness fathered her, so darkness will mother her until a new day, a rebirth.

Comedic Resolution

Directions: Read the following poem and analyze the patterns of images and symbols. Consider the categories provided below.

A Refusal to Mourn the Death, by Fire, of a Child in London

Never until the mankind making
Bird beast and flower
Fathering and all humbling darkness
Tells with silence the last light breaking
And the still hour
Is come of the sea tumbling in harness

And I must enter again the round
Zion of the water bead
And the synagogue of the ear of corn
Shall I let pray the shadow of a sound
Or sow my salt seed
In the least valley of sackcloth to mourn

The majesty and burning of the child's death.
I shall not murder
The mankind of her going with a grave truth
Nor blaspheme down the stations of the breath
With any further
Elegy of innocence and youth.

Deep with the first dead lies London's daughter,
Robed in the long friends,
The grains beyond age, the dark veins of her mother,
Secret by the unmourning water
Of the riding Thames.
After the first death, there is no other.

—Dylan Thomas

1. Consider recurrences of these images:

    light/darkness

    nature

    sound

    water

    human activity

2. How do biblical allusions provide a symbolic framework for the poem?

3. How can the poem be classified as a comedic elegy? In what sense is it an anti-elegy?

Lesson 26

Evaluation

Objective

- To evaluate the mastery of the concepts of this unit in a simulation comparable to the Advanced Placement Examination

Notes to the Teacher

At this point, students should be able to take "delight in disorder" (knowing that it is really order) when they read any poem. They should know what pattterns are for and recognize their presence even when they do not dominate the surface of the poem. They should also be in a position to appreciate variations of patterns. It is only a matter of time until students can encounter poems such as those by Dylan Thomas, E. E. Cummings, Wallace Stevens, and John Donne without feeling threatened by syntactical and metaphorical complexity.

Procedure

1. Administer the examination on **Handout 45** within a regular class period (45-50 minutes). Suggest 15-20 minutes for the objective section and 30 minutes for the essay.

2. Answers for Part I:
   1. d 2. d 3. e 4. d 5. b 6. d 7. a

3. Suggested Responses for Part II:
   Answers should include some of the following observations.

The speaker reveals himself to the reader as a person overwhelmed with hatred for a confrere, Brother Lawrence. A complete focus of the speaker's attention on the activity of this brother results in a psychological study of obsession.

Due to a lack of any additional details, we assume that the speaker's motive is one of jealousy. He conforms to the pretenses of piety ("Knife and fork. . . crosswise. . . in Jesu's praise"), while Brother Lawrence, who does not, is regarded by others as a saint.

The speaker, not content to find fault with Brother Lawrence's behavior (small talk at table, cleanliness, success as a gardener, etc.), uses his imagination to place him in compromising positions: the presence of young women, the possession of a "scrofulous French novel," or even heresy (Manichean) and Satan's "indenture."

The speaker's words and syntax alternate between intimate and formal. Usually the intimate voice of the speaker is confined to the thoughts reserved to himself. His mocking comments and rhetorical questions are more formal and are usually followed by a more personalized aside ("He-he! There his lily snaps!") This fluctuation between private and public discourse and diction reinforces the ironic tone of the poem, which results from the "double image" of the hypocritical speaker.

Evaluation

Directions: The following examination is a simulation of the Advanced Placement Examination in English Literature and Composition. The time-frame has been adjusted so that you may complete it in one testing period. You should complete Part I in less than fifteen minutes and dedicate the remainder of the time to the completion of the essay in Part II.

Part I

"Soliloquy of the Spanish Cloister"

Read the following poem and answer the quesitons which follow. You may need the following explanations of allusions in the poem.

"Salve tibi!": a Latin greeting; Hello!

Barbary corsair: a pirate of the Barbary coast in North Africa

Arian: subscriber to a heretical view that claimed Christ was not God, thus denying the Trinity

Abbot: the head of a cloister (monastery or abbey)

Galatians: an epistle by Paul in the Christian Scriptures

Manichee: subscriber to a heresy

French novel: for several centuries the British viewed the French as models of immorality

Hy, Zy, Hine: echoes of a Germanic curse . . . as far back as Marlowe's play, *Doctor Faustus* (the Renaissance), selling one's soul to the devil took place in a German setting

Vespers: evening prayers

"Plena gratia,/Ave, Virgo!": Hail Virgin, full of grace (from Vespers, a prayer which was chanted in honor of the Virgin Mary)

Soliloquy of the Spanish Cloister

GR-R-R—there go, my heart's abhorrence!
    Water your damned flower-pots, do!
If hate killed men, Brother Lawrence,
    God's blood, would not mine kill you!
What? your myrtle-bush wants trimming?
    Oh, that rose has prior claims—
Needs its leaden vase filled brimming?
    Hell dry you up with its flames!

II

At the meal we sit together:
    Salve tibi! I must hear
Wise talk of the kind of weather,
    Sort of season, time of year:
Not a plenteous cork-crop: scarcely
    Dare we hope oak-galls, I doubt:
What's the Latin name for "parsley"?
    What's the Greek name for Swine's Snout?

III

Whee! We'll have our platter burnished,
    Laid with care on our own shelf!
With a fire-new spoon we're furnished,
    And a goblet for ourself,
Rinsed like something sacrificial
    Ere 'tis fit to touch our chaps—
Marked with L. for our initial!
    (He, he! There his lily snaps!)

IV

Saint, forsooth! While brown Dolores
    Squats outside the Convent bank,
With Sanchicha, telling stories,
    Steeping tresses in the tank,
Blue-black, lustrous, thick like horsehairs,
    —Can't I see his dead eye glow
Bright, as 'twere a Barbary corsair's?
    (That is, if he'd let it show!)

V

When he finishes refection,
  Knife and fork he never lays
Cross-wise, to my recollection,
  As do I, in Jesu's praise.
I, the Trinity illustrate,
  Drinking watered orange-pulp—
In three sips the Arian frustrate;
  While he drains his at one gulp!

VI

Oh, those melons! If he's able
  We're to have a feast; so nice!
One goes to the Abbot's table,
  All of us get each a slice.
How go on your flowers? None double?
  Not one fruit-sort can you spy?
Strange!—And I, too, at such trouble,
  Keep 'em close-nipped on the sly!

VII

There's a great text in Galatians,
  Once you trip on it, entails
Twenty-nine distinct damnations,
  One sure, if another fails.
If I trip him just a-dying,
  Sure of Heaven as sure can be,
Spin him round and send him flying
  Off to Hell, a Manichee?

VIII

Or, my scrofulous French novel,
  On grey paper with blunt type!
Simply glance at it, you grovel
  Hand and foot in Belial's gripe:
If I double down its pages
  At the woeful sixteenth print,
When he gathers his greengages,
  Ope a sieve and slip it in't?

IX

Or, there's Satan!—one might venture
   Pledge one's soul to him, yet leave
Such a flaw in the indenture
   As he'd miss till, past retrieve,
Blasted lay that rose-acacia
   We're so proud of! *Hy, Zy, Hine. . .*
'St, there's Vespers! *Plena gratia*
   Ave, Virgo! Gr-r-r—you swine!

—Robert Browning

( ) 1. From the details provided in the poem, we can conclude that the speaker:
    a. is a wise and holy person
    b. has a justified opinion of Brother Lawrence
    c. is very candid and makes his feelings known to everyone
    d. is jealous of Brother Lawrence
    e. is favored by the abbot

( ) 2. The speaker reflects his "worldliness" in all except one of the following:
    a. his curses
    b. his possession of a "scrofulous French novel"
    c. his attention to Dolores and Sanchicha
    d. his knowledge of the *Epistle to the Galatians*
    e. his lack of Christian charity

( ) 3. The form of the poem is achieved by:
    a. the use of heroic couplets
    b. blank verse
    c. eight-line stanzas in iambic pentameter
    d. ballad stanzas
    e. octaves rhyming abab, cdcd

( ) 4. The tonal structure of the poem is achieved by all except one of the following:
    a. the alternate sarcasm and pietism of the speaker
    b. the contrast between the speaker's pretenses and real feelings
    c. the ironic use of cloister setting
    d. the extensive use of figurative language
    e. the occasional variation in meter for emphasis

( ) 5. The genre of the poem can best be described as:
    a. tragic
    b. satiric
    c. comedic
    d. romantic
    e. both satiric and comedic

( ) 6. The speaker expresses his hatred for Brother Lawrence in all except one of the following ways:
    a. by direct statement of fact
    b. by attempting to sabotage his fruit crop
    c. by fantasy: proving to him, on his deathbed, that he is a Manichee, a heretic
    d. by crossing knife and fork at table, an obvious attempt to place a curse on him
    e. by thinking about placing an indecent book where Brother Lawrence will find it

( ) 7. The speaker finds fault with all except one of the following qualities of Brother Lawrence:
    a. He is the gardener.
    b. He engages in small talk at table.
    c. He is neat.

d. He does not engage in pious, symbolic acts, e.g., drink his beverage in three sips in honor of the Trinity.

e. He is considered saintly.

Part II: Essay

Any literary text requires a reader to rely upon the observations of others in order to acquire the necessary information to enter the imaginary world of the work. In Browning's "Soliloquy of the Spanish Cloister," the reader has access to only one voice. In a well-developed essay, evaluate the role of the speaker as a reliable guide in the world of this poem. Take into account the psychological context of his speech: a) motives; b) perceptions; c) emotions; and d) behavior, and the ways in which they are communicated by the diction, syntax, and tone of the entire poem.

Part IV
Critical Perspectives

An Advanced Placement English program must provide multiple opportunities for students to experience and respond to significant literary texts in a variety of ways. The experience of the text challenges students to activate their analytical skills; they need a forum in which they can respond. Class discussions allow for a free exchange of ideas among peers as well as with teachers.

Journal writing, short critical papers and essay tests provide an opportunity for more formulated expression. Still another source of insight can be the selective reading of literary criticism.

Students should not be encouraged to read literary critics until they have gained a certain measure of self-confidence in their own ability to respond as critics. They should be warned that critics are "professional" readers and evaluators and that many of their insights are the result of years of study, often of a single author's works.

Louise Rosenblatt has provided an accurate guideline with which to deal with literary criticism.

> Coming to the critic after one's own transaction with the text, one can be helped to realize more keenly the character of that experience. Like other readers, critics may reveal the text's potentialities for responses different—perhaps more sensitive and more complex— from our own. The critic may have developed a fuller and more articulate awareness of the literary, ethical, social, or philosophic concepts that he brings to the literary transaction, and may thus provide us with a basis for uncovering the assumptions underlying our own responses. In this way, critics may function not as stultifying models to be echoed but as teachers, stimulating us to grow in our own capacities to participate creatively and self-critically in literary transactions. . .
>
> Superseded then is the image of the critic presenting "the work" as a self-contained object which he is, with almost scientific assurance, describing for us. Instead, he comes to us as a fellow reader who has gone through the arduous process of creating a literary work from a text, with all the implied personal involvement, trial-and-error ordering of responses, frustrations, and fulfillments. Criticisms addressed to the general reader should reflect more of the dynamics of a reading, reporting it as an event in time, in a particular personal or environing context. Moving in this direction, some critics today do articulate the attitudes and experiences they bring to the text. Or at least they alert us to assumptions or systematic approaches that enter into their critical activities. In a sense, this requires that the critic help us both to participate in the particular work he has evoked from the text, and also to understand his reflections on his concurrent responses to that work.[1]

[1]*The Reader, The Text, The Poem* (Southern Illinois University Press, 1978), pp. 148–49.

Lesson 27

Textual Truth and Aesthetic Beauty

Objectives

- To demonstrate the role of textual variations in the interpretation of a poem
- To further explore the philosophical considerations evoked by a poem

Notes to the Teacher

As mentioned in Lesson 23, few lines in poetry have received more critical attention than the concluding lines of Keat's "Ode on a Grecian Urn":

'Beauty is truth, truth beauty,' —that is all
Ye know on earth, and all ye need to know.

The lines form a concluding comment to what has become a very famous poem. The innate ambiguity of the lines has been further complicated by the fact that different manuscripts yield three differently punctuated versions of these final two lines. The result is a variety of interpretations of the lines, as well as of the relationship they bear to the rest of the poem.

Students benefit from such an inquiry into textual variation and its syntactical consequences.

Procedures

1. Review the text of the poem, **Handout 12**.

2. Discuss the problem posed by the variations in text as stated on **Handout 46, Part I**.

3. Have students compare their conclusions with those in Part II of the handout. You may ask one or several students to research and report to the class the problem in greater detail according to the sources listed in Stillinger's Appendix to *Twentieth Century Interpretations of Keats' Odes.*

Name _____

Date _____

The Truth of Beauty

Part I

Different manuscripts of Keats's "Ode on a Grecian Urn" give three different versions of the final two lines of the poem. They are as follows:

1. Beauty is Truth, —Truth Beauty,—that is all
     Ye know on earth, and all ye need to know.
2. Beauty is Truth, Truth Beauty. —That is all
     Ye know on Earth, and all ye need to know.
3. "Beauty is truth, truth beauty,"—that is all
     Ye know on earth, and all ye need to know.

As you can observe, the differences in punctuation result not only in differences of speaker and addressee, but also in a difference in what is actually said. Taking these three textual variations into account, what different interpretations of the final two lines are possible:

1. if the lines are spoken by the poet to the reader?

2. if the lines are spoken by the poet to the urn?

3. if the lines are spoken by the poet to figures on the urn?

4. if the lines are spoken by the urn to the reader?

Part II: Read the following critical comments and compare them to your own ideas.

Who Says What to Whom at the End of
Ode on a Grecian Urn?

Interpretation of the final lines of *Ode on a Grecian Urn* has frequently turned on the specific questions of who speaks the last thirteen words, and to whom. The textual evidence is inconclusive (see *PMLA*, LXXIII [1958], 447–48); each of the following versions has a claim to authority:

Beauty is Truth,—Truth Beauty,—that is all
    Ye know on earth, and all ye need to know.
        (consensus of four transcripts; capitalization varies)

Beauty is Truth, Truth Beauty.—That is all
    Ye know on Earth, and all ye need to know.
        (*Annals of the Fine Arts, for MDCCCXIX,*
                publ. c. Jan., 1820)

"Beauty is truth, truth beauty,"—that is all
    Ye know on earth, and all ye need to know.
        (Keats's *Lamia* volume, publ. July, 1820)

No single explanation can satisfy the demands of text, grammar, dramatic consistency, and common sense. But critics do tend to stand on single explanations, and it may therefore be useful to summarize briefly the various possibilities, along with the objections usually raised against each.

(1) *Poet to reader:* The poet, commenting on the urn's "message," says "that is all/Ye know on earth, and all ye need to know" to the reader (and thereby to mankind generally). This is a common older interpretation which, like (2) and (3) below, is based at least initially on the *Lamia* volume's use of quotation marks to separate "Beauty . . . beauty" from the rest of the two lines. J. M. Murry, *Keats* (1955), pp. 210–26, is a typical proponent of the view. *Objections:* The reader and man have become "us" and "ours" in the final stanza; the poet's shift of address to "ye" would be both inconsistent and unprepared for (he has not earlier spoken directly to the reader/mankind). Then there is the question of meaning. At face value, the statement is false to everybody's experience of life—as one unsympathetic reader put it, "Beauty ain't truth and truth ain't beauty and you've got to know a helluva lot more than that on earth." (Critics of course have to go past face value. Victor M. Hamm, *Explicator,* III [1945], item 56, paraphrases, "That is all you [anyone comtemplating the urn] know about the urn, and all you need to know," and reads the lines as a reply to the unanswered questions posed in the first and fourth stanzas.)

The explanation by Earl Wasserman, *The Finer Tone* (1953), p. 60, should be included under this heading: the poet's words to the reader, "that . . . know," refer not only to the urn's "message" but to the three lines preceding—"When old age . . . ." An additional objection here is the obscurity of reference, since few readers, unaided, would grasp the intended scope of "that."

(2) *Poet to urn:* This is a minority view that continues to be put forward—see William R. Wood, *English Journal*, XXIX (1940), 837–39; Roy P. Basler, *Explicator*, IV (1945), item 6; Porter Williams, Jr., *Modern Language Notes*, LXX (1955), 342–45; and especially Martin Halpern, *College English*, XXIV (1963), 284–88. The poet's final words are read as a comment on the urn's limitations: in Basler's paraphrase, "That is all you . . . know, and all you need to know; but, I know a great deal more, and a different quality of beauty and truth." *Objections:* "Ye" is normally a plural pronoun. And the urn has been referred to as "thou" throughout the poem. (Halpern cites instances of singular "ye," as well as shifts of pronouns, elsewhere in Keats's poems. A number of critics suggest that Keats may have changed pronouns to avoid the cacophony of "that is all/Thou knowest on earth, and all thou needest to know.") "On earth" in the last line is meaningless if applied to the urn.

(3) *Poet to figures on the urn:* This (proposed by G. St. Quintin, *Times Literary Supplement*, February 5, 1938, p. 92, and more recently by Robert Berkelman, *South Atlantic Quarterly*, LVII [1958], 354–58) is a variety of the preceding, but better accords with the normal use of "ye" as a plural. *Objections:* The figures are not "on earth." Moreover, the poet has ceased to think of them as alive and capable of hearing; he is again addressing the urn as artifact, and the images of the last stanza emphasize the lifelessness of "marble men and maidens." And there is no reason why the figures should know only "Beauty . . . beauty," or anything at all.

(4) *Urn to reader:* The commonest view of the conclusion of the ode—popularized by Cleanth Brooks and C. M. Bowra in the 1940's, reinforced by the solid stand of the Harvard Keatsians, Douglas Bush, W. J. Bate, and David Perkins, and seemingly sanctioned by the punctuation in the transcripts—has the urn speaking the whole of the last two lines. *Objections:* There is again the question of common-sense meaning (though it seems better for the urn to tell us what we know and need to know than for the poet to do so). The principal obstacle, however, is the punctuation of the text in the *Lamia* volume. Several critics (e.g., R. D. Havens, *Modern Philology*, XXIV [1926], 213; Leo Spitzer, *Comparative Literature*, VII [1955], 220–21) have suggested that the quotation marks may have been intended to set off "Beauty . . . beauty" as an apothegm, motto, or sepulchral epigram. Bush (e.g., in his *Selected Poems and Letters, 1959*) and others, rejecting the *Lamia* punctuation, simply move the closing quotation mark to the end of the poem.

From Jack Stillinger, ed., Appendix to *Twentieth Century Interpretations of Keats's Odes* (Prentice Hall, Englewood Cliffs, NJ, 1968).

Lesson 28
Paradox and Poetry

Objectives

- To explore the role of paradox in the poetic process
- To collaborate with an established critical perspective on the use of paradox

Notes to the Teacher

In the introductory chapter of his formidable collection of critical essays, The *Well Wrought Urn*, Cleanth Brooks makes the case for paradox and poetry:

> Our prejudices force us to regard paradox as intellectual rather than emotional, clever rather than profound, rational rather than divinely irrational . . . Yet there is a sense in which paradox is the language appropriate and inevitable to poetry. It is the scientist whose truth requires a language purged of every trace of paradox; apparently the truth which the poet utters can be approached only in terms of paradox.[1]

Few poems fulfill this expectation more than John Donne's "The Canonization," a poem that "can be approached only in terms of paradox." It exposes students to the full range of poetic perceptions.

To complete this lesson, you will need one or more copies of *The Well Wrought Urn*.

Procedures

1. Distribute **Handout 47.** Read the poems to the students, or play recorded versions. Allow students to respond to the poems informally. Direct the students to consider:
   the speakers   the symbolism
   the subjects   the tones
   the dominant metaphors   the diction

2. Have students complete **Handout 47,** Part II, on the basis of their understanding of the poems.

3. Direct one or several students to read Chapter One of *The Well Wrought Urn* and record Mr. Brooks' insights on **Handout 47.**

4. Conduct a group discussion in which students consider both their own insights and Mr. Brooks' ideas. Encourage students to test the validity of those answers in contrast to the responses that the rest of the class has listed. Emphasize the fact that answers should be evaluated in relation to the text and to the extent that they provide greater understanding of it. Criticism is not totally a consideration of "right" and "wrong."

Suggested Responses may include the following observations:

1. *We tend to think of poetry as "the language of the soul" or emotion. Paradox, in contrast, is associated with the "intellectual rather than emotional." Poetry, in order to be effective, must incorporate both emotion and intellect.*

2. *The poet is "filled with worship, but the girl who walks beside him is not." The poet's enthusiasm is momentary; hers is "all the year." The evening's beauty is visible, public, "as a nun"; the girl's is within, beyond appearances."*

3. *The statement is rather commonplace and the descriptive details are very general, even impressionistic.*

4. *The speaker is surprised when he realizes that the city is a part of nature also.*

5. *The poet deals with both human and divine love, which are often viewed very differently.*

6. *It is a "parody of Christian sainthood; but it is an intensely serious parody. . ." Donne is not mocking religion but uses the basic paradox of the poem to draw love and religion closer together.*

[1]Cleanth Brooks, *The Well Wrought Urn* (Harcourt, Brace and World, 1947), 3.

7. In terms of the metaphorical level, it is the "secular world which the lovers have renounced."

8. Politics and business

9. The tone shifts from irritation to an ironic awareness of the paradoxical nature of love.

10. The metaphors in the second stanza are the exaggerated figures of the Petrarchan tradition, but by the third stanza the reader is alert to the mocking use of the conventions. "The poet points out to his friend the infinite fund of such absurdities which can be applied to lovers:

   Call her one, me another flye,
   We are tapers too, and at our owne cost die
   . . .

   In the final two stanzas the metaphors are serious and precise. The irony is in reference to the secular world which now looks to the phoenix and the saints of love as a model.

11. Tombs, epitaphs, legends, chronicles, half-acre tombs are all means of public display. As the speaker points out:

   We can dye by it, if not live by love.

   The death of love is associated with the private world of verse (the sonnet) and ashes are committed to "a well wrought urn." The paradox is in the reversal. By their death to the public world they will become a model for it. Their ashes, like those of the phoenix, will be the source of a new life.

5. The best way to fulfill the objectives of this lesson is to have students demonstrate their understanding of the role of paradox by an independent analysis of a poem in which they focus on the use of paradox. Additional research may be completed in *The Well Wrought Urn* as well. Additional chapters include

   a. selections from Shakespeare's MACBETH in "The Naked Babe and the Cloak of Manliness"

   b. The Light Symbolism in "L'Allegro-Il Penseroso" (by Milton)

   c. "What Does Poetry Communicate?" (a consideration of Robert Herrick's "Corinna's Going a Maying")

   d. "The Case of Miss Arabella Fermor" (on Pope's "The Rape of the Lock")

   e. "Gray's Storied Urn" (on Gray's "Elegy Written in a Country Churchyard")

   f. "Wordsworth and the Paradox of the Imagination" (on "Ode: Intimations of Immortality from Recollections of Early Childhood")

   g. "Keats' Sylvan Historian: History without Footnotes" (on "Ode on a Grecian Urn")

   h. "The Motivation of Tennyson's Weeper" (on "Tears, Idle Tears")

   i. "Yeats' Great Rooted Blossomer" (on "Among School Children")

Name _____

Date _____

Poetry and Paradox

Part I: Read these poems, and respond to their speakers, subjects, figurative language, tone, and diction.

It Is a Beauteous Evening

It is a beauteous evening, calm and free,
The holy time is quiet as a Nun
Breathless with adoration; the broad sun
Is sinking down in its tranquillity;
The gentleness of heaven broods o'er the Sea:
Listen! the mighty Being is awake,
And doth with his eternal motion make
A sound like thunder—everlastingly.
Dear Child! dear Girl; that walkest with me here,
If thou appear untouched by solemn thought,
Thy nature is not therefore less divine:
Thou liest in Abraham's bosom all the year;
And worshipp'st at the temple's inner shrine,
God being with thee when we know it not.

—William Wordsworth

Composed upon Westminster Bridge, September 3, 1802

Earth has not anything to show more fair:
Dull would he be of soul who could pass by
A sight so touching in its majesty:
This City now doth, like a garment, wear
The beauty of the morning; silent, bare,
Ships, towers, domes, theaters, and temples lie
Open unto the fields, and to the sky;
All bright and glittering in the smokeless air.
Never did sun more beautifully steep
In his first splendor, valley, rock, or hill;
Ne'er saw I, never felt, a calm so deep!
The river glideth at his own sweet will:
Dear God! the very houses seem asleep;
And all that mighty heart is lying still!

—William Wordsworth

The Canonization

For God's sake, hold your tongue, and let me love,
   Or chide my palsy, or my gout,
My five gray hairs, or ruined fortune flout,
    With wealth your state, your mind with arts improve,
      Take you a course, get you a place,   5
      Observe his Honor, or his Grace,
Or the King's real, or his stamped face
   Contemplate; what you will, approve,
   So you will let me love.

Alas, alas, who's injured by my love?   10
   What merchant's ships have my sighs drowned?
Who says my tears have overflowed his ground?
    When did my colds a forward spring remove?
   When did the heats which my veins fill
    Add one more to the plaguy bill?   15
Soldiers find wars, and lawyers find out still
   Litigious men, which quarrels move.
   Though she and I do love.

Call us what you will, we are made such by love;
   Call her one, me another fly.   20
We are tapers too, and at our own cost die,
    And we in us find the eagle and the dove,
    The phoenix riddle hath more wit
By us; we two being one, are it.
So to one neutral thing both sexes fit.   25
   We die and rise the same, and prove
   Mysterious by this love.

We can die by it, if not live by love,
   And if unfit for tombs and hearse
Our legend be, it will be fit for verse;   30
    And if no piece of chronicle we prove,
     We'll build in sonnets pretty rooms;
     As well a well-wrought urn becomes
The greatest ashes, as half-acre tombs.
    And by these hymns, all shall approve   35
    Us canonized for love:

And thus invoke us; "You whom reverend love
   Made one another's hermitage;
You, to whom love was peace, that now is rage;
   Who did the whole world's soul contract, and   40
      drove
   Into the glasses of your eyes
     (So made such mirrors and such spies.
That they did all to you epitomize)
   Countries, towns, courts: beg from above
   A pattern of your love!"   45

               —John Donne

Part II: Answer the following questions based on your understanding of paradox and how it is employed in the poems on this handout.

1. What is paradoxical about the statement: ". . . the language of poetry is the language of paradox"?

2. What paradox is evident in Wordsworth's sonnet "It is A Beauteous Evening, Calm and Free"?

3. Why is it difficult to account for Wordsworth's sonnet, "Composed upon Westminster Bridge," in terms of "nobility of sentiment" and "brilliance of its images," two expectations often brought to the appreciation of poetry?

4. What accounts for this poem's quality or "goodness"?

5. How does the basic metaphor of John Donne's "Canonization" involve a paradox?

6. In what sense is "The Canonization" a parody?

7. In terms of the metaphorical level of the poem, who is the addressee?

8. What are the "categories of secular success" that the speaker recommends to the addressee?

9. How does the tone of the poem shift before the conclusion?

10. What similarities and differences are evident in the extravagant love-metaphors as the poem progresses?

11. Divide the following words from the poem into two categories and explain your classification based on the context in which they are used in the poem:

tombs	verse
epitaph	legend
chronicle	sonnets
urn	half-acre tombs

Lesson 29

Critical Perspectives

Objectives

- To outline the major tenets of various schools of modern criticism
- To familiarize students with the variety of critical approaches which allows for enrichment in literary study

Notes to the Teacher

The critical "prejudice" of the preceeding lessons has been an emphasis on formalistic and reader-response approaches to literary analysis. However, students of literature should be familiar with a variety of critical approaches. This exposure will prepare them for reading and sorting out the emphases which they encounter as they read various critics, as well as provide them with additional insights and approaches as they initiate their own critical inquiries.

In his masterful treatment of romantic theory, *The Mirror and the Lamp*, M. H. Abrams establishes a flexible frame of reference for relating various critical theories to each other. He notes that there are four elements (the artist, the universe, from which is derived the subject, the audience, and the work itself) which all literary theories incorporate. He visualizes these four co-ordinates in a triangular relationship.

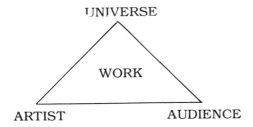

He notes:

> Although any reasonably adequate theory takes some account of all four elements, almost all theories, as we shall see, exhibit a discernible orientation toward one only. (p. 6)

Procedures

1. Discuss the need for critical response to everything within our experience in the context of the intellectual satisfaction which this process of demystification provides. Focus on the primary function of art (i.e., entertainment) and the fact that a greater understanding of art in any form leads to increased appreciation and enjoyment.

2. Draw Abrams' paradigm (see Notes) on the chalkboard and explain the various elements. Perhaps the following quotation will clarify his distinctions:

> Four elements in the total situation of a work of art are discriminated and made salient, by one or another synonym, in almost all theories which aim to be comprehensive. First, there is the *work*, the artistic product itself. And since this is a human product, an artifact, the second common element is the artificer, the *artist*. Third, the work is taken to have a subject which, directly or deviously, is derived from existing things—to be about, or signify, or reflect something which either is, or bears some relation to, an objective state of affairs. This third element, whether held to consist of people and actions, ideas and feelings, material things and events, or super-sensible essences, has frequently been denoted by that word-of-all-work, 'nature'; but let us use the more neutral and comprehensive term, *universe*, instead. For the final element we have the *audience*: the listeners, spectators, or readers to whom the work is addressed, or to whose attention, at any rate, it becomes available. (p. 6)

3. Distribute **Handout 48** and review the basic tenets of each school of criticism.

The Critic's Choice

Directions: Four elements are involved in the process which produces art: the artist, the universe which provides the subject for the work of art, the audience or the reader, and the work itself, the product of the process. Examine the following summary of ideas of various schools of criticism, each of which tends to place special importance on the role of a single element in the artistic process. As you review these summaries and consider their potential limitations, think of specific poems which you have read that best appeal to these approaches. Do you feel that any one approach is better than another? Formulate your own literary theory.

Focus on the Artist

1. *BIOGRAPHICAL CRITICISM*
   a. Position: The poem reflects the events, specific experiences, prejudices, and "truths" of the poet's personal life. Often lyric poetry and/or poetry written in the first person is interpreted as autobiographical. Occasional narrative poems are viewed as thinly disguised biographies.
   b. Consideration: The danger inherent in this approach is the fallacious assumption that the poet cannot create a voice other than his/her own and incorporate experiences which are fictional. A poem may be autobiographical but is not necessarily so. It may also be a combination of factual and fictional experience.

2. *PSYCHOLOGICAL CRITICISM*
   a. Position: The poem reflects the psychological state of the poet and is a manifestation of his/her expressed or repressed needs, desires, ambitions, frustrations, etc.
   b. Consideration: All poetry to some extent reflects the felt and rationalized experiences of the poet. However, to deny a poet the power to imagine and emote is to deny the nature of creativity which is the catalyst for poetic expression. Poems by poets whose lifestyle and poetic style were controversial (e.g., Poe, Whitman, Dickinson, Plath) are often singled out for consideration by psychological critics. Psychological analysis is often unfairly confused with bizarre and deviant behavior, since much psychological criticism has been derived from the theories of Sigmund Freud. In truth, all poetry has a psychological dimension by necessity since it reflects the emotional and rational state of the artist which produced it.

Focus on the Universe

1. *SOCIOLOGICAL/HISTORICAL CRITICISM*
   a. Position: The poem expresses the values, issues and concerns of the age which produced it.
   b. Consideration: Poetry is the mirror of its age but the reflection which it produces may not always be realistic. All literature arrives at its "truth" by comparison, irony, understatement, exaggeration. To equate poetic fact with historical fact is to distort the truth of both. Poetry often responds to the issues of an age, but the nature of that response is universal. It transcends the limitations of sociological insight and the propaganda of the here-and-now. Poetry often reflects the dictates

191

and tastes of literary history in diverse ways: the Renaissance sonnet; the meta-physical, cavalier, neo-classical, romantic movements; the modern taste for ten-sion, paradox, free verse. The efforts of poets to experiment with form and genre have all been the result of the impact of literary history on the history of poetry.

2. *MORALISTIC/DIDACTIC CRITICISM*
   a. Position: Poetry reflects (or should reflect) a higher truth, an ethical perspective; it teaches the reader how to live and behave.
   b. Consideration: Poetry, although it reflects values, is nonsectarian. A poem does not cease to be a poem because it does not reflect your values or those of your na-tion, culture, religion or politics. You may object to its message, but a poem is more than what it means in a literal sense.

Focus on the Audience

READER-RESPONSE CRITICISM
   a. Position: The poem is recreated each time by its reader and can only mean what the individual reader or a community of readers brings to bear on its interpreta-tion. This transaction process will result in an ongoing refinement of meaning, meaning-in-process. There is no interpretation which *every* reader can share in at any point in the process.
   b. Consideration: The "affective fallacy," which this approach implies, results from the assumption that because the reader *feels* something the work *means* some-thing. The impressions of the reader are the criteria for criticism. There is no such thing as objectivity.

Focus on the Work

1. *PHILOSOPHICAL CRITICISM*
   a. Position: The poem is a reflection of great ideas and should be related to intellectu-al history.
   b. Consideration: To say that poetry = ideas is to say that poetry = philosophy. If this is true, why write or read poetry? Is poetry "what oft was thought, but ne'er so well ex-pressed" as Alexander Pope maintained, or is it just a summary of great ideas?

2. *LINGUISTIC CRITICISM*
   a. Position: Poetry is a process of communication. Consequently, we must study the resources of language, the meanings of individual words and their syntactical pat-terns, in order to better understand the communicated message.
   b. Consideration: If this is true, how does a poem differ from prose? What makes po-etic discourse unique?

3. *FORMALISTIC CRITICISM*
   a. Position: Poetry is an artful arrangement of language characterized by formal ele-ments which separate it from the language of ordinary (grammatical) or even persua-sive (rhetorical) discourse. It is necessary to analyze it in terms of *how* (technique) the language is given shape, how the formal elements result in an aesthetic effect.
   b. Consideration: The search for aesthetic meaning is ultimately a human, hence a social activity, and cannot be isolated in the world of the poetic work. A poem's "art" only makes sense in the context of its inception (by its artist) and reception (by its audience).

Lesson 30
Practical Criticism

Objective

- To apply various critical approaches to poems familiar to students

Notes to the Teacher

In his introduction to *Practical Criticism*, a landmark experiment in the psychology of criticism, I. A. Richards warns that the "one and only goal of all critical endeavours . . . is improvement in communication . . . The whole apparatus of critical rules and principles is a means to the attainment of finer, more precise, more discriminating communication." He notes that the evaluation process which criticism anticipates will usually be settled if the mental condition (i.e., greater understanding) is established. He also warns the student-critic (and the teacher):

> Critical principles, in fact need wary handling. They can never be a substitute for discernment though they may assist us to avoid unnecessary blunders . . . Everything turns upon how the principles are applied. It is to be feared that critical formulas, even the best, are responsible for more bad judgments than good, because it is far easier to forget their subtle sense and apply them crudely than to remember it and apply them finely. (pp. 10–11)

The student-critic should be cautioned to avoid dogmatic interpretation and be open to the variety of ways that a poem may be perceived.

Procedures

1. Distribute **Handout 49.** This worksheet may be used as a guideline for classroom discussion, small group activity, or as an independent assignment. Have students use it in conjunction with **Handout 48** ("The Critic's Choice") as well as texts of poems on **Handouts 1, 10, 12, 14, 15, 20 and 23.**

2. Answers will, of course, vary. Emphasize that students' critical responses are more important than their applications of specific critical theories. A theory is just a way of providing focus and approaching a greater understanding of the poetic text.

3. After students have had the opportunity to read and respond to **Handout 49,** distribute **Handout 50.** Review and discuss model responses, comparing them with those which the students have formulated.

Name _____

Date _____

Critical Response

Directions: Review the poems indicated and answer the questions according to the critical perspective implied.

1. What points would a sociological critic emphasize about "Norman Morrison" by Adrian Mitchell (**Handout 1**)?

2. What points would a moralistic critic emphasize about "Nobody Comes" by Thomas Hardy (**Handout 10**)?

3. What points would a reader-response critic emphasize about John Keats' "Ode on a Grecian Urn" (**Handout 12**)?

4. What points would a formalistic critic emphasize about John Updike's "Player Piano" (**Handout 14**)?

5. What points would a psychological critic emphasize about Bruce Springsteen's "The Promised Land" (**Handout 15**)?

6. What points would a linguistic critic emphasize about John Donne's "A Lecture upon the Shadow" (**Handout 20**)?

7. What points would a philosophical critic emphasize about John Milton's "On the Late Massacre in Piedmont" (**Handout 24**)?

Name _____

Date _____

Critical Response Models

1. "Norman Morrison" by Adrian Mitchell (**Handout 1**): As a product of the turbulent 1960's, this poem echoes the discontent and disillusionment of the age. It is anti-establishment in its sarcastic tone ("the white heart of Washington where everyone could see" is ironically contrasted with the "dark corners of Vietnam where nobody could see"). It implies a rejection of "United beautiful States of terrible America" citizenship as he burned himself and "his passport" and "became Vietnamese." The social comment of the poem dominates and may even distract from its artistic unity of effect. (sociological approach)

2. "Nobody Comes" by Thomas Hardy (**Handout 10**): The moral of this poem is arrived at by implication. The theme touches on the isolation and loneliness which result from living in a world that "has nothing to do with me." The cause for physical and psychological separation from society is not stated, but blame must be placed on either the individual or the society which allows this condition to exist. "No man is an island. . ." (moralistic approach)

3. "Ode on a Grecian Urn" by John Keats (**Handout 12**): Although many aspects of this poem inspire consideration, the line in Section V in which the speaker, in reference to the urn, notes that it "dost tease us out of thought/As doth eternity," is especially provocative. The urn has many things about it which tease us to think. The poem's initial metaphor of the "unravished bride of quietness" offers a paradoxical consideration. The unanswered questions of Section I will never have historical answers. The "unheard melodies" are "sweeter" but only to the imagination, not to reason or the senses. Perhaps the teasing thoughts which the urn does provoke are also the cause for teasing "us out of thought." We can imagine eternity in some metaphorical way but never rationally respond to it since it is alien to the content of our experience. Therefore, the "message" of the urn (and of eternity) can "tease us out of thought," i.e., take away our reasoning ability. However, to experience this form of insanity is not undesirable according to the context provided. The urn will remain "a friend to man" for future generations and teach beauty's truth, "all ye need to know." (reader-response)

4. "Player Piano" by John Updike (**Handout 14**): The poem is unified by the personification of the piano. The fact that the piano also functions as the speaker helps to establish the humorous tone. The sound structure completes the personification, as cacophony and alliteration echo the honky-tonk "sense" of the piece. (formalistic approach)

5. "The Promised Land" by Bruce Springsteen (**Handout 15**): The speaker of these lyrics is psychologically prepared for confrontation. Although he is "just killing time" with work and "chasing some mirage" with play, he expresses the desire to "take charge." Although he expresses his hopes for the future to some unidentified "little girl," he moves on to assert his manhood ("I ain't a boy, no, I'm a man") to "Mister," to whom he reveals his belief in a "promised land." "Pretty soon" becomes *now* and he is "heading straight into the storm" to test his faith and realize his unfulfilled dreams.

197

However, by his statements and his actions, he reveals that he will be rewarded for his efforts "to live the right way" and for his faith in a better life ("promised land"). (psychological approach)

6. "A Lecture upon the Shadow" by John Donne (**Handout 20**): The speaker implies that the addressee is in need of a lecture on "Love's philosophy." Such an assumption is as redundant as the preceding phrase when viewed in terms of the etymological word play that the poet employs. A lecture, from the Latin *lex*, is literally a reading, the format employed in medieval and renaissance universities where books were scarce and women were not present. In Greek, *philos* means "love" and *sophos* means "wisdom." This wisdom of love is, however, something that a person cannot stand still for and be lectured about; it is always "growing" and "love's day is short." Therefore, the philosophy of love which the poem's language implies is imbedded in the paradox of time and the effort of the speaker to control it (and the education of his beloved). (linguistic approach)

7. "On the Late Massacre in Piedmont" by John Milton (**Handout 24**): In an effort to find significance in the death of "slaughtered saints," the speaker does not just appeal to God for revenge. He also examines the long term effects which this incident will cause. He anticipates the "hundredfold" harvest of true believers which the martyred "blood and ashes" of those slain will generate. Likewise, in philosophical fashion, he reasons that this new generation will be better prepared to avoid the forces of evil which threaten even the future (the "Babylonian woe"). (philosophical approach)

Lesson 31
Critical Dispositions

Objectives

- To get acquainted with a variety of critical approaches as employed by professional critics
- To examine the "high seriousness" of literary criticism through a parody of its approach

Notes to the Teacher

A healthy respect for the opinions of others is an important part of each student's intellectual growth. This attitude can be fostered by classroom discussions and various forms of peer/teacher interaction. Likewise, a healthy skepticism is equally important. No idea should be rejected or accepted before it is carefully examined. The same attitude is applicable to students' approach to literary criticism. While they should recognize and respect the experience of critics and teachers, they should be encouraged to question, reexamine, and respond to all that is presented to them under the guise of "objective truth." When they see themselves as members of a community of readers, they understand that literary criticism is an accumulation of educated opinion that must be examined for its values, emphasis, possibilities, and limitations.

Procedures

1. Distribute **Handout 51.** Ask students to identify the critical position which each passage demonstrates and their reasons for such conclusions. They may wish to use **Handout 48** ("The Critic's Choice") to aid them in this procedure.

Suggested Responses:

1. *Formalistic approach: The critic finds fault with the use of poetry as a vehicle for communicating "certain feelings about social justice" (antisociological) and feels that the poem uses "mass language" in order to achieve this effect rather than take advantage of the form and technique of poetic discourse.*
2. *Reader-response approach: The constant references to the reader and the dynamic reading process by which meaning is discerned are clues to this critical approach.*
3. *Linguistic approach: The etymological examination and the consequent analysis of wordplay are of special interest to the linguistic critic.*
4. *Psychological approach: The Freudian emphasis and the psychoanalytic interpretation of parable are indicators of this approach.*
5. *Sociological/Historical approach: The passage attempts to make a connection between "disorder" in both dress and society.*

2. Distribute **Handout 52.** Students will not have much difficulty in reading the essay. They will sense its humor in general but may be at a loss to identify its causes. The study questions should help them understand its techniques a little better.

Suggested Responses:

1. a. "prose demand" = meaning
    b. "proto-response" = first reaction
    c. in medias res = in the middle of things, not providing background at the outset (characteristic of most epics)

2. The poet manipulates the reader's "proto-response" in order to achieve poetic truth.

3. The poet "prepares us" by altering the sequence of the seasons and easing us into their tragic decline.

4. The correct authors are Oedipus Rex-Sophocles; "The Illiad"—Homer; "The Aeneid—Vergil. This mocks the formalistic approach which cannot be "bothered" with any extrinsic information in the interpretation of a poem.

5. The critic seems to think that the word is capitalized for emphasis; in fact it is capitalized because it begins a new line (poetic convention).

6. It is rather farfetched to think that the "X" sound of "excepting" causes all of these connotative responses on the part of the reader.

7. He personifies months and makes February the tragic hero, a symbol of individualism.

8. No, Tantalus was punished for his disobedience to the gods by being placed in a pool, which would recede each time that he attempted to drink, and near fruits which would move beyond his grasp as he reached for them. This is the mythical etymology of "tantalize." It was Ixion who was punished by being stretched on a wheel. The purpose of this distorted simile is to underscore the formalist's seeming lack of knowledge of external information.

9. The author parodies the formalistic school, with its emphasis on patterns, relationships, tone (sensibility), tension, ambiguity, and a tendency to be circumloquacious.

10. According to earlier investigations (see Lesson 4), poetry is "language charged with meaning," language which "suggests," language which gives "pleasure by its form, as distinct from its matter." This parody has tried to use the language of criticism to "charge" the language of verse with an energy that it can hardly sustain. Some students will still be confused by these distinctions if they have been more attentive to the language of criticism than the language of poems. Most, however, will detect the "put-on" that the parody presents.

Name _____

Date _____

Critical Variations

1. Review Edna St. Vincent Millay's "Justice Denied in Massachusetts" (Lesson 2, **Handout 4**) before you read the following critical comments.

> What from the splendid dead
> We have inherited—
> Furrows sweet to the grain, and the weed subdued—
> See now the slug and the mildew plunder.
> Evil does overwhelm
> The larkspur and the corn;
> We have seen them go under.

From this stanza by Miss Millay we infer that her splendid ancestors made the earth a good place that has somehow gone bad—and you get the reason from the title: "Justice Denied in Massachusetts." How Massachusetts could cause a general dessication, why (as we are told in a footnote to the poem) the execution of Sacco and Vanzetti should have anything to do with the rotting of the crops, it is never made clear. These lines are mass language: they arouse an affective state in one set of terms, and suddenly an object quite unrelated to those terms gets the benefit of it; and this effect, which is usually achieved, as I think it is here, without conscious effort, is sentimentality. Miss Millay's poem was admired when it first appeared about ten years ago, and is no doubt still admired, by persons to whom it communicates certain feelings about social justice, by persons for whom the lines are the occasion of feeling shared by them and the poet. But if you do not share those feelings, as I happen not to share them in the images of dessicated nature, the lines and even the entire poem are impenetrably obscure.

(from "Tensions in Poetry" by Allen Tate)

2. from *A Reader's Guide to Contemporary Literary Theory* (Raman Selden, p. 108) Consider the following poem by Wordsworth:

> A slumber did my spirit seal;
> I had no human fears;
> She seemed a thing that could not feel
> The touch of earthly years.
>
> No motion has she now, no force;
> She neither hears nor sees;
> Rolled round in earth's diurnal course,
> With rocks, and stones, and trees.

Leaving aside many preliminary and often unconscious steps which readers must make to recognise that they are reading a lyric poem, and that they accept the speaker as the authentic voice of the poet and not as a dramatic persona, we can say that there are two 'statements' made, one in each stanza: (i) I thought she could not die; (ii) She is dead. As readers we ask ourselves what sense we make of the *relationship* between the statements. Our interpretation of every phrase will turn on the answer to this question. How are we to regard the speaker's attitude towards his earlier thoughts about the female (baby, girl, or woman)? Is it good and sensible to have 'no human fears', or is it naive and foolish? Is the 'slumber' which sealed his spirit a sleep of illusion or an inspired reverie? Does 'she seemed' suggest that she had all the visible marks of an immoral being, or that the speaker was perhaps mistaken? Does the second stanza suggest that she has no spiritual existence in death and is reduced to mere inanimate matter? The first two lines of the stanza invite this view. However, the last two lines open another possible interpretation—that she has become part of a natural world and partakes of an existence which is in some sense grander than the naive spirituality of stanza one; her individual 'motion' and 'force' is now subsumed in the grand motion and force of Nature.

3. Review John Donne's "The Canonization" (Lesson 28, **Handout 47**) before reading the following comments from *The Explicator Cyclopedia*, Vol. II, p. 100.

The current interpretation of line 7 is Cleanth Brooks': "The two main categories of secular success are neatly, and contemptuously epitomized . . . . Cultivate the court and gaze at the king's face there, or . . . get into business and look at his face stamped on a coin" (*The Well Wrought Urn*, p. 10). The key word *reall* does mean "actual" here, but another applicable meaning negates the conclusion that the line "neatly" epitomizes "two main categories." The *reall* is a Spanish coin, etymologically the *royal* coin, often bearing the king's image. Donne must have known the *reall* in Spain or in England before he wrote "The Canonization." Since the monetary signification is quite appropriate, it must be assumed that he intended a double meaning. This assumption is supported by the position the word holds in the history of the language and in Donne's vocabulary. This line is the earliest *NED* example of *reall* in the sense "the actual (thing or person)," and it is the only occurrence of *reall* in Donne's poetry. Donne may well have forced the sense of *reall* to create the wordplay. The line then has two meanings: "the king's actual face and his face on a coin," and "the king's royal coin, his stamped face." The latter meaning contains no separation into "categories," and when both meanings are apprehended simultaneously, as they should be, a complex fusion of both categories is created.

March 1955 —Lewis Sawin

4. from *A Handbook of Critical Approaches to Literature*, p. 109.

"The Sick Rose"

O rose, thou art sick!
 The invisible worm,
That flies in the night,
 In the howling storm,

Has found out thy bed
 Of crimson joy;
And his dark secret love
 Does thy life destroy.

From the Freudian perspective, the sexual implications of Blake's imagery are fairly discernible. The rose is a classic symbol of feminine beauty. But this beauty is being despoiled by some agent of masculine sexuality: the worm, symbol of death, of decay, and also of the phallus (worm = serpent = sexual instinct). . .we encounter the metaphor of flying, Freudian symbol of sexual pleasure. Images of night, darkness, and howling storm suggest attributes of the unconscious or the Id . . . The second stanza sets forth in rather explicit images the idea of sensual destruction. In short, Blake's poem is a vaguely disturbing parable of the death-instinct which psychoanalysts affirm is so closely conjoined with sexual passion. The sharp juxtaposition of "crimson joy" and "destroy" (coupled with "bed" and "his dark secret love") suggests that Eros, unmitigated by higher spiritual love, is the agent of evil as well as of mortality.

5. from *English Poetry and the English Language*, p. 29

Delight in Disorder

A sweet disorder in the dress
Kindles in clothes a wantonness;
A lawn about the shoulders thrown
Into a fine distraction;
An erring lace, which here and
there
Enthralls the crimson stomacher;
A cuff neglectful, and thereby
Ribands to flow confusedly;
A winning wave (deserving note)
In the tempestuous petticoat;
A careless shoe-string, in whose tie
I see a wild civility:
Do more bewitch me, than when art
Is too precise in every part.

Robert Herrick

The impression of a surprising richness, and almost grandeur (as of a painting by Titian), with a certain tantalizing quality, that Herrick's poem leaves, is primarily due to the skill with which he has exploited the ambiguous associations of the epithets. On the surface his subject is the "Delight in the Disorder" of the title—a disorder, that is, of costume. But a second subject is hinted at, though not protruded: a delight in disorder, not of costume but of manners and morals. It is not only the clothes but their wearers too whom he would have *sweet, wanton, distracted, erring, neglectful, winning, tempestuous, wild,* and *bewitching* rather than *precise*. The poem, in fact, instead of being the mere *jeu d'esprit* that it would seem to be, is essentially a plea for paganism. There are three themes: (1) untidiness is becoming; (2) the clothes are the woman; (3) anti-Puritanism. But the success of the poem depends upon the fact that the themes are not isolated and contrasted but grow out of and into each other. The suspension between the various meanings produces a range of reference that none of them would have alone.

Name _____

Date _____

How to Criticize a Poem[1]
(In the Manner of Certain Contemporary Critics)

1.

I PROPOSE to examine the following poem:

> Thirty days hath September,
> April, June and November:
> All the rest have thirty-one,
> Excepting February alone,
> Which has only eight and a score
> Till leap-year gives it one day more.

2.

The previous critics who have studied this poem, Coleridge among them, have failed to explain what we may describe as its fundamental *dynamic.* This I now propose to do. The first thing to observe is the order in which the names (or verbal constructs) of the months are presented. According to the prose meaning—what I shall henceforth call the prose-*demand*—"September" should not precede, it should follow "April," as a glance at the calendar will show. Indeed "September" should follow not only "April," it should also follow "June" if the prose-demand is to be properly satisfied. The prose order of the first two lines should therefore read: "Thirty days hath April, June, September and November." That is the only sequence consonant with prose logic.

3.

Why then, we ask ourselves, did the poet violate what educated readers know to be the facts? Was he ignorant of the calendar, believing that September preceded April in the progress of the seasons? It is difficult to imagine that such was the case. We must find another explanation. It is here that the principle of dynamic analysis comes to our aid.

4.

Dynamic analysis proves that the most successful poetry achieves its effect by producing an *expectation* in the reader's mind before his sensibility is fully prepared to receive the full impact of the poem. The reader makes a *proto-response* which preconditions him to the total response toward which his fully equilibrized organs of apperception subconsciously tend. It is this proto-response which the poet has here so sensitively manipulated. The ordinary reader, trained only to prose-demands, expects the usual order of the months. But the poet's sensibility knows the poetic truth is more immediately effective than the truth of literal chronology. He does not *state* the inevitable sequence; he *prepares* us for it. In his profound analysis of the two varieties of mensual time, he puts the *gentlest* month first. (Notice how the harsh sound of "pt" in "September" is softened by the "e" sound on either side of it.) It is the month in which vegetation first begins to fade, but which does not as yet give us a sense of tragic fatality.

[1]Theodore Spencer, "How to Criticize a Poem," *The New Republic,* December 6, 1943.

5.

Hence the poet prepares us, dynamically, for what is to follow. By beginning his list of the months *in medias res,* he is enabled to return later to the beginning of the series of contrasts which is the subject of his poem. The analogy to the "Oedipus Rex" of Euripides and the "Iliad" of Dante at once becomes clear. Recent criticism has only too often failed to observe that these works also illustrate the dynamic method by beginning in the middle of things. It is a striking fact, hitherto (I believe) unnoticed, that a Latin poem called the "Aeneid" does much the same thing. We expect the author of that poem to begin with the departure of his hero from Troy, just as we expect the author of our poem to begin with "April." But in neither case is our expectation fulfilled. Cato, the author of the "Aeneid," creates dynamic suspense by beginning with Aeneas in Carthage; our anonymous poet treats his readers' sensibilities in a similar fashion by beginning with "September," and then *going back* to "April" and "June."

6.

But the sensibility of the poet does not stop at this point. Having described what is true of *four* months, he disposes of *seven* more with masterly economy. In a series of pungent constructs his sensibility sums up their inexorable limitations: they *All* (the capitalization should be noted) "have thirty-one." The poet's sensibility communicates a feeling to the sensibility of the reader so that the sensibility of both, with reference to their previous but independent sensibilities, is fused into that momentary communion of sensibility which is the final sensibility that poetry can give both to the sensibility of the poet and the sensibility of the reader. The texture and structure of the poem have erupted into a major reaction. The ambiguity of equilibrium is achieved.

7.

Against these two groups of spatial, temporal and numerical measurements—one consisting of four months, the other of seven—the tragic individual, the sole exception, "February," is dramatically placed. February is "alone," is cut off from communion with his fellows. The tragic note is struck the moment "February" is mentioned. For the initial sound of the word "excepting" is "X," and as that sound strikes the sensibility of the reader's ear a number of associations subconsciously accumulate. We think of the spot, the murderous and lonely spot, which "X" has so frequently marked; we remember the examinations of our childhood where the wrong answers were implacably signaled with "X"; we think of ex-kings and exile, of lonely crossroads and executions, of the inexorable anonymity of those who cannot sign their names. . . .

8.

And yet the poet gives us one ray of hope, though it eventually proves to be illusory. The lonely "February" (notice how the "alone" in line four is echoed by the "only" in line five), the solitary and maladjusted individual who is obviously the hero and crucial figure of the poem, is not condemned to the routine which his fellows, in their different ways, must forever obey. Like Hamlet, he has a capacity for change. He is a symbol of individualism, and the rhythm of the lines which are devoted to him signalize a gayety, however desperate, which immediately wins our sympathy and reverberates profoundly in our sensibility.

9.

But (and this is the illusion to which I have previously referred) in spite of all his variety, his capacity for change, "February" cannot quite accomplish (and in this his tragedy consists) the *quantitative* value of the society in which circumstances have put him. No matter how often he may alternate from twenty-eight to twenty-nine (the poet, with his exquisite sensibility, does not actually *mention* those humiliating numbers), he can never achieve the bourgeois, if anonymous, security of "thirty-one," nor equal the more modest and aristocratic assurance of "thirty." Decade after decade, century after century, millennium after millennium, he is eternally frustrated. The only symbol of change in a changeless society, he is continually beaten down. Once every four years he tries to rise, to achieve the high, if delusive, level of his dreams. But he fails. He is always one day short, and the three years before the recurrence of his next effort are a sad interval in which the remembrance of previous disappointment melts into the futility of hope, only to sink back once more into the frustration of despair. Like Tantalus he is forever stretched upon a wheel.

10.

So far I have been concerned chiefly with the dynamic *analysis* of the poem. Further study should reveal the *synthesis* which can be made on the basis of the analysis which my thesis has tentatively attempted to bring to an emphasis. This, perhaps, the reader with a proper sensibility can achieve for himself.

THEODORE SPENCER

Study Questions

1. What, according to their contents, are:
   a. "prose-demand"
   b. a proto-response
   c. *in medias res*

2. How does the poet's "sensitivity" and "sensibility" impact upon the poem, according to the critic?

3. How did the poet "prepare us" for the "inevitable sequence" of the seasons?

4. Is the critic always correct in designating the authorship of literary works? What accounts for any inaccuracies?

5. Why does the critic state that "the capitalization should be noted for "All"? What is the real reason for capitalization?

6. The "insight" of Section 7 is derived from an assumption on the part of the critic. What is that assumption? Is it believable or far-fetched? Why?

7. What literary technique has the critic imposed on his description of the poem which does not seem to be utilized in the poem?

8. Was Tantalus stretched on a wheel? What is the source of this allusion/simile? Why is it distorted?

9. What critical approach does the critic seem to parody and how?

10. Is the poem a poem? Why or why not?

Lesson 32

Playing the Role of the Critic: All the World's an Audience

Objective

- To provide students with the opportunity to function as a critic, to explain to others the significance of a poetic text.

Notes to the Teacher

It is important to avoid imposing "teacher prejudice" in the process of educating student-critics. Most of us are confirmed in our critical perspectives and think we see through the limitations of other positions. Students, however, need to experience first hand the process of discovery, acceptance, or rejection of what others have to say. Otherwise, they will learn very early in the "investigation" that the "teacheristic approach" is the only one worth considering and will prepare themselves right away to give you back what you want to hear. To allow a student the opportunity to reason and react independently is more important than producing ghost writers or disciples for Cleanth Brooks, Stanley Fish, Irving Babbitt, or Joseph Wood Krutch.

Procedures

1. Distribute **Handout 53** ("How Now?"). Have students work together as a class or in small groups as they read and discuss the poems.

   Suggested Responses:
   1. *"Rhymes for John Grimes" by Samuel Hazo*
      Biographical: The author attended Notre Dame (Indiana) in the late 1940s. The references to "teacher's courses" and "collegiate girls" would lead us to conclude that John Grimes was a college friend.
      Philosophical: We are always influenced by our past ("remembrance never ends" and "your words have never narrowed to a close") and, when it is remembered, it "is now."

   2. *"The Beautiful Changes" by Richard Wilbur*
      Reader-response: Although this approach must begin with the reader and not be limited by any given rubric, most readers will respond in terms of the "kind ways" that nature uses to transform beauty and the way that the imagination responds to it ("wonder"). The imagination unifies and transforms the beauty in nature and the beauty of the addressee.

   3. *"For the Anniversary of My Father's Death" by Maggie Anderson:*
      Psychological: The speaker ritualistically comes to terms with a father's death after one year: "decay," both literal (the coffin, the body) and psychological ("You are harder to see now"), brings about a realization that those left behind must go on living ("This new year will begin with my hands steady . . . I will speak"). The poem has been something of an exorcism of the father's spirit, but at the same time a beginning and an ending: "This is the first song; this is the last song. This is the last song for you."

2. Distribute **Handout 54.** Ask students to select one poem and one critical approach as the focus of a written or oral report for some assigned, future date. Students may need some time (perhaps two weeks) to do research for some poems if they choose certain critical approaches (e.g., biographical, historical, etc.). Many of the poems are frequently anthologized; others may require students to seek individual volumes of poems by the poets. This latter activity is, in itself, an educational experience, for students often think of a poet's complete works in terms of the few selections which are encountered in an anthology.

This listing may also serve two additional purposes:

1. For the student, it may serve as an independent reading list, a means of gaining directed access to some of the best poems written in the English language.

2. For the teacher, it provides a supplementary list of very teachable poems, representing a variety of themes, periods, forms, styles and authors.

Name _____

Date _____

How Now?

Directions: After a careful reading of the following poems, indicate what aspects of each poem suggest the use of the listed critical approaches. Quote key phrases when possible and explain your conclusions.

1.

Rhymes for John Grimes

In fifteen years I never wrote to you
at all nor you to me, but what is true

of brothers can be truer still of friends.
In either case remembrance never ends.

Without a card to bring us up to date
since our last talk in nineteen forty-eight,

your words have never narrowed to a close.
The past is when we read each other's prose

or when you laughed and said your uncle ran
in Birmingham as a Republican

and tallied just a single vote—his own.
The past is when you wanted to be shown

real snow or when we questioned over beer
what urged Van Gogh to razor off his ear

and give it boxed in tissue to a tart.
Waiting for football Saturdays to start

is past, and biting apples while we walked
against an Indiana wind and talked

of how one teacher's courses changed our lives
or if collegiate girls could make good wives.

The more we talked, the more we learned to say
what makes me realize that life today

is living up to what we said we knew.
Of all our books and teachers, just a few

reminded us to be the men we are,
and they, like you, have kept me right so far

that I have linked these lines to prove just how
the past, when we remember it, is now.

Samuel Hazo

Biographical:

Philosophical:

2.

The Beautiful Changes

One wading a Fall meadow finds on all sides
The Queen Anne's Lace lying like lilies
On water; it glides
So from the walker, it turns
Dry grass to a lake, as the slightest shade of you
Valleys my mind in fabulous blue Lucernes.

The beautiful changes as a forest is changed
By a chameleon's tuning his skin to it;
As a mantis, arranged
On a green leaf, grows
Into it, makes the leaf leafier, and proves
Any greenness is deeper than anyone knows.

Your hands hold roses always in a way that says
They are not only yours; the beautiful changes
In such kind ways,
Wishing ever to sunder
Things and things' selves for a second finding, to lose
For a moment all that it touches back to wonder.

Richard Wilbur

Reader-response:

For the Anniversary of My

Father's Death

3.

Today is the last time I shall speak to you.
Now I shall cease speaking to you, my relative.
—from a Fox Indian chant to the dead

It has been one year. The wood on your casket must have started to decay. There is a stone at the head of your grave for safe passage of your soul, and poinsettias from my uncle, your brother, who wishes you that.

You, dead, in your blue suit, on a mattress and pillow, with those brown spots on your hands, around your mouth and eyes. You are harder to see now. Someone else lives in your house.

But I can still see large plates with birds on them. They are arranged around a table, with a brown lace tablecloth, waiting for friends to arrive. There will be a party. And I can see sweat stains on a brown chair, a red bathrobe, two red pencils on a formica tabletop, three blue candles, a pile of newspapers, a black umbrella. Still, I tell you, my father, I will not die yet.

This new year will begin with my hands steady; the energy begins in my feet. There is a wheel above my left eye that has started to turn again. I will speak. This is the first song; this is the last song. This is the last song for you.

—Maggie Anderson

Psychological:

Name _____

Date _____

All the World's a Poem: A Select Reading List

Auden, W. H.	"Anthem for St. Cecilia's Day"
	"As I Walked Out One Evening"
	"In Memory of William Butler Yeats"
	"Musee des Beaux Arts"
Arnold, Matthew	"Dover Beach"
	"Stanzas from the Grand Chartreuse"
Anonymous	"Bonnie Barbara Allen"
	"The Wife of Usher's Well"
	"Get Up and Bar the Door"
Ashbery, John	"A Man of Words"
Barker, George	"To My Mother"
Bishop, Elizabeth	"Visit to St. Elizabeth's"
Browning, Robert	"Parting at Morning"
	"Meeting at Night"
Blake, William	"The Garden of Love"
	"Infant Sorrow"
	"The Tiger"
	"I Saw a Chapel All of Gold"
	"Mock On, Mock On"
	"And Did Those Feet"
	"Holy Thursday"
	"The Sick Rose"
	"The Poison Tree"
Byron, Lord, George Gordon	"Sonnet on Chion"
	"So We'll Go No More A-Roving"
Croso, Gregory	"Marriage"
Coleridge, Samuel Taylor	"Kubla Khan"
	"The Rime of the Ancient Mariner"
	"Dejection: An Ode"
Ciardi, John	"The Gift"
Crane, Hart	"Voyages II"
Cummings, E. E.	"anyone lived in a pretty how town"
	"pity this busy monster manunkind not"
	"the Cambridge ladies"
	"when serpents bargain for the right to squirm"
	"next to of course god america i"
Dickinson, Emily	"At Half Past Three, A Single Bird"
	"I'll Tell You How the Sun Rose"
	"My Life Had Stood—A Loaded Gun"
	"Safe in Their Alabaster Chambers"
	"The Soul Selects Her Own Society"
	"There's A Certain Slant of Light"

214

Name _____

Date _____

"These Are the Days When Birds Come Back"

"I Taste a Liquor Never Brewed"

"There Came A Day at Summer's Full"

"After Great Pain, A Formal Feeling Comes"

"I Heard a Fly Buzz—When I Died"

"This World Is Not Conclusion"

"I Started Early—Took My Dog"

"Because I Could Not Stop for Death"

"Further In Summer Than The Birds"

"A Route Of Evanescence"

Donne, John

"The Anniversarie"

"A Valediction: Forbidding Mourning"

"Good Friday 1613: Riding Westward"

"At the Round Earth's Imagined Corners"

"Death Be Not Proud"

"Batter My Heart, Three Personed God"

Dryden, John

"Hymn for St. Cecilia's Day"

Eberhart, Richard

"The Groundhog"

Eliot, T. S.

"Gerontian"

"The Hippopotamus"

"The Hollow Men"

"Journey of the Magi"

"Preludes"

"The Love Song of J. Alfred Prufrock"

Frost, Robert

"The Rose Family"

"The Death of the Hired Man"

"Mending Wall"

"Birches"

"Provide, Provide"

"The Silken Tent"

"The Road Not Taken"

"Acquainted With The Night"

"Two Tramps in Mud Time"

"Stopping By Woods On A Snowy Evening"

"West Running Brook"

"Fire and Ice"

"After Apple Picking"

Ferlinghetti, Lawrence

"Truth is Not the Secret of a Few"

"Constantly Risking Absurdity"

Ginsberg, Allen

"A Supermarket in California"

"Sunflower Sutra"

Gunn, Thom

"Black Jackets"

"Taylor Street"

Gray, Thomas

"Elegy Written in a Country Churchyard"

Graves, Robert

"The Naked and the Nude"

Hardy, Thomas   "Neutral Tones"

"The Man He Killed"

"The Subalternas"

"Satires of Circumstances"

"The Darkling Thrush"

"Church Monuments"

Hecht, Anthony   "More Light! More Light"

"Third Avenue in Sunlight"

"The Dover Bitch"

Hughes, Ted   "Pike"

"Hawk Roosting"

Hopkins, Gerard Manley   "The Caged Skylark"

"The Habit of Perfection"

"God's Grandeur"

"Spring and Fall"

"The Windhover"

"Pied Beauty"

Herbert, George   "The Pilgrimage"

"The Pulley"

"Jordan I & II"

Herrick, Robert   "Corinna's Going A-Maying"

"The Funeral Rites of the Rose"

Housman, A. E.   "Farewell to Barn and Stack and Tree"

"Loveliest of Trees"

"On Wenlock Edge"

"To an Athlete Dying Young"

"With Rue My Heart Is Laden"

Jonson, Ben   "Still to be Neat"

"On My First Son"

Jarrell, Randall   "The Woman at the Washington Zoo"

Justice, Donald   "But That Is Another Story"

X. J. Kennedy   "Nude Descending A Staircase"

Kinnell, Galway   "Burning"

Koch, Kenneth   "Permanently"

Keats, John   "Ode on Melancholy"

"To Autumn"

"Ode to A Nightingale"

"The Eve of St. Agnes"

Larkin, Philip   "Poetry of Departure"

Levertov, Denise   "To the Reader"

Lowell, Robert   "For the Union Dead"

"Mr Edwards and the Spider"

"Skunk Hour"

Longfellow, Henry Wadsworth   "The Jewish Cemetery at Newport"

Lovelace, Richard   "To Lucasta, Going to tne wars"

"To Althea, from Prison"

Moore, Marianne

"The Student"

"Poetry"

MacLeish, Archibald

"Ars Poetica"

"Not Marble, Nor the Gilded Monument"

"Dover Beach—a Note on That Poem"

"You, Andrew Marvell"

Marvell, Andrew

"Bermudas"

"To His Coy Mistress"

"The Garden"

"The Definition of Love"

Milton, John

"Lycidas"

"On the Morning of Christ's Nativity"

Owen, Wilfred

"Arms and the Boy"

"Anthem for Doomed Youth"

"Disabled"

Pound, Ezra

"Hugh Selwyn Mauberley"

Poe, Edgar Allan

"Ulalume"

"The City in the Sea"

Roethke, Theodore

"Elegy for Jane"

"The Waking"

"Infirmity"

Ransom John Crowe

"Bells for John Whiteside's Daughter"

Robinson, Edgar Arlington

"Miniver Cheevy"

"Mr. Flood's Party"

Raleigh, Sir Walter

"The Lie"

"His Pilgrimage"

"What Is Our Life?"

Spenser, Edmund

"One Day I Wrote Her Name upon the Strand"

Sexton, Anne

"The Moss of His Skin"

Shapiro, Karl

"Auto Wreck"

Stevens, Wallace

"The Anecdote of the Jar"

"The Comedian as the Letter C"

"A High-toned Old Christian Woman"

"Peter Quince at the Clavier"

"Sunday Morning"

"Thirteen Ways of Looking at a Blackbird"

Stafford, William

"Traveling Through the Dark"

Sassoon, Siegfried

"Base Details"

Shakespeare, William

"Shall I Compare Thee to a Summer's Day?"

"When, in Disgrace with Fortune and Men's Eyes"

"When to the Sessions of Sweet Silent Thought"

"Not Marble, nor the Gilded Monuments"

"That Time of Year Thou Mayst in Me Behold"

"When I do Count the Clock that Tells the Time"

"Like as the Waves Make Toward the Pebbled Shore"

"Farewell! Thou Art Too Dear for My Possessing"

"When in the Chronicles of Wasted Time"

"Let Me Not to the Marriage of True Minds"

"Poor Soul, the Centre of My Sinful Earth"

Thomas, Dylan

"Fern Hill"

"The Force That Through the Green Fuse"

"In My Craft and Sullen Art"

Taylor, Edward

"Huswifery"

Tennyson, Alfred, Lord

"Ulysses"

"Tears, Idle Tears"

Wilbur, Richard

"Love Calls Us to The Things of This World"

"On the Marginal Way"

Whitman, Walt

"When Lilacs Last in the Dooryard Bloomed"

Wilde, Oscar

"The Ballad of Reading Gaol"

Wordsworth, William

"London, 1802"

"The Solitary Reaper"

"Ode: Intimations of Immortality"

"Tintern Abbey"

"It Is A Beauteous Evening, Calm and Free"

"Lines Composed upon Westminster Bridge"

"The World is Too Much with Us"

"A Slumber Did My Spirit Seal"

Yeats, William Butler

"The Lake Isle of Innisfree"

"Sailing to Byzantium"

"Among School Children"

"A Dialogue of Self and Soul"

"Adam's Curse"

"Leda and the Swan"

"The Second Coming"

"When You are Old"

"The Wild Swans at Coole"

"An Irish Airman Forsees His Death"

Lesson 33
The Heresy of Paraphrase

Objective

- To return students' attention to the need to understand poetry and all literature as more than the summary of its parts

Notes to the Teacher

In order to prepare students for an extended use of critical sources in a research assignment, it may be timely to reemphasize some very fundamental considerations:

- A poem is more than *what* it "says": its story, moral or message.
- A poem's art culminates in *how* technique is applied and "fits" the resources of language.
- The true poem is always more than all of the things that can be said about it. It is a gift that keeps on giving.

If students are not alert to this, they will tend to go symbol hunting or to be content to rush to critical resources and let others think for them. Research should follow only careful reading and extended consideration of the original text.

Procedures

1. The "world" of *The Rape of the Lock* is very far removed in time and texture from our own experience. We have supplemented our understanding of eighteenth century drawing room society (which is the subject as well as the originally intended audience for the poem) with the facts of its history and the artificats of its culture. For a greater appreciation of the poem, students benefit from exposure to portraits of ladies by Gainsborough, the music of Mozart or Handel, some understanding of how the "idle rich" utilized their leisure, and the impact of the neo-classical movement on literature, art, architecture, and the philosophy of the age. Attempt to fill in such gaps in students' background to the extent that need and time allow. (Note: Handel's "Water Music" works well to create the mood of Belinda " 'midst attending dames/Launched on the bosom of the silver Thames" (ll.19–20) as does his "Fireworks Music" with the conclusion (ll.168–182), as "the beau monde shall from the mall survey" the star which was once Belinda's hair, and "hail with music its propitious ray.")

2. Distribute **Handout 55.** Have students read the prose summary in preparation for an oral reading of the poem. The version of the text here is Pope's earliest, so it will not match most recordings which use later revisions. Read the entire poem to the students so that they will hear its stately rhythms, clever rhymes, and dramatic effects. Do not pause for comment or discussion. Ask students to note any parts that they want to question for clarification.

3. At the conclusion of the reading ask students to describe their reactions to both the prose summary and the poem. Attention will probably focus on Pope's use of the heroic couplet, irony, satirical techniques, and characterization. If students have any experience of epic poetry, they may notice the parody of style. Do not attempt to give the discussion too much direction of closure. Allow students to digress, but use the text as a focal point. The next lesson attempts to summarize the discussion and provide additional insight.

The Prose of the Poem

Directions: Read the following prose summary of Alexander Pope's *The Rape of the Lock*. Be particularly attentive to details which would otherwise serve as footnotes to the poem itself. This will help you to appreciate the poem when you read it and not distract you from its total impact. Be prepared to discuss the different effects that the two versions have on you.

In Summary

Alexander Pope's *The Rape of the Lock* (1712) is a satirical poem written in response to an actual occurrence. A feud between two aristocratic families ensued when an acquaintance of Pope, Lord Petre, clipped a lock of hair from the head of a certain Arabella Fermor. At the suggestion of his friend, John Caryll (1.3), Pope transformed the event into a mock-heroic epic in two cantos. Later revisions expanded this format, but the original version is used here.

The poem begins, in the epic tradition, with an invocation of the muse for inspiration and a statement of the poem's moral (l. 1–2). Following a series of rhetorical questions (ll. 8–13), the scene is established. Sol (the sun) arouses "the gentle belle" (Belinda) from her sleep and she readies herself for a boat trip on the river Thames (through London). Belinda is much admired for her beauty (ll. 21–29), but her "tragic flaw" ("if belles had faults to hide") is her bold display of "two locks" of hair which are like "labyrinths," "springes" (bird traps), or fishlines (thin lines, like hairs, used to catch the "finney prey," or fish). A young Baron "Resolved to win" and "By force to ravish" the "bright locks", and prays to Phoebus Apollo, the sun god, and Venus, the goddess of love (ll. 49–62), to whom he sacrifices "all the trophies of his former loves" (Sylvia's gift of ribbons for his sword and Flavia's corset support or "busk," and various "billet-doux" or love letters). All meet at Hampton Court ("a structure of majestic frame" where Queen Anne takes both counsel and tea) to pass "the cheerful hours" with tea, cards and gossip (ll. 63–94). The Baron discovers "new stratagems" and ignores the precedent of Scylla's mythical fate when she caused the destruction of a kingdom by plucking out one of the hairs from the head of her father, Nisus. The Baron is aided by a "lady in waiting," Clarissa, who provides the "little engine" (the forfex or scissors) used to "divide . . . the sacred hair" (ll. 95–116) The triumphant Baron seizes his prize (like the ancient Greeks, a victor wears a wreath) and feels that his name will live on (as long as melodramatic love novels such as *Atlantis* are read or social visits are made by society women). If steel destroyed Troy, should not the hairs of "fair nymphs" be conquered by "unresisted steel" (ll. 117–140)?

In Canto II, Belinda's "rage, resentment and despair" are detailed. Her friend, Thalestris (named after the queen of the Amazon women warriors) urges her to retaliate. After "constant care" of her hair with "bodkins" (hair pins), pomatums (a mousse or gel), and curling techniques (wrapping in paper), is she to be humiliated by her "ravisher" who will "display this hair" in a ring for all to see (ll. 1–22)? It would be better for "grass to grow in Hyde Park Circus (a well travelled road), for "wits" to live in Bow (an unfashionable area), or the "earth. . .men, monkeys . . . perish all" than to be the "degraded toast" of society (ll.

23–40). Thalestris sends Sir Plume to the Baron as an intermediary, but the Baron ignores his entreaties. Belinda herself appears, regretting the fact that she ever entered into fashionable society. At least she could have preserved her lost lock if she had "unadmired remained/In some lone isle . . . where none learn ombre" (cards) or "taste bohea" (a kind of tea) (ll. 41–78). She had ignored the various warnings (e.g. "thrice . . . the patchbox fell," the box of silk patches used to cover facial blemishes), and feels that the remaining lock of hair will experience the same "fate." The Baron's ears are deaf to all pleas, even more than Aeneas ("the Trojan") to the loved-pleas of Dido and her sister, Anna, on her behalf (ll, 79–95). Thalestris gives a call "to arms." and an epic, drawing room battle ensues. As in Homer, "all Olympus rings with loud alarms" (the gods choose sides). Belinda attacks the Baron with "a charge of snuff." In the midst of the battle, however, the lock "In every place is sought, but sought in vain." Heaven has judged that "with such a prize no mortal must be blessed" (ll. 96–155). Some speculate that it is "mounted in the lunar sphere" (where other mortal "treasures" abound, such as books which engage in "hair-splitting arguments," i.e., tomes of casuistry). The muse, with her "quick poetic eyes" (like Proculus, who saw Romulus ascend into the heavens), saw the lock turn into a shooting star with "a radiant trail of hair," brighter than "Bernice's Hair," a comet named after an Egyptian queen of the third century B.C Now fashionable society (the "beau monde") shall be able to see Belinda's lock of hair as they walk in the park ("mall"). Even the eighteenth century astrologer, John Partridge, will be able to see it through the telescope ("Galileo's eyes") and, as he was inclined to do each year, predict the downfall of the king of France (Louis) and the papacy of Rome (ll. 156–182). Belinda should no longer mourn the loss since the lock now "adds new glory" to the heavens and assures her immortality, long after "all those tresses shall be laid in dust" (ll. 183–192).

The Poem Itself

The Rape of the Lock

Canto I

What dire offense from amorous causes springs,
What mighty quarrels rise from trivial things,
I sing—This verse to C—1, Muse! is due;
This, even Belinda may vouchsafe to view:
Slight is the subject, but not so the praise,   5
If she inspire, and he approve my lays.
   Say what strange motive, goddess! could compel
A well-bred lord t'assault a gentle belle?
Oh say what stranger cause, yet unexplored,
Could make a gentle belle reject a lord?   10
And dwells such rage in softest bosoms then?
And lodge such daring souls in little men?
   Sol through white curtains did his beams display,
And oped those eyes which brighter shine than they;
Shock just had given himself the rousing shake,   15
And nymphs prepared their chocolate to take;
Thrice the wrought slipper knocked against the ground,
And striking watches the tenth hour resound.
Belinda rose, and 'midst attending dames
Launched on the bosom of the silver Thames: 20
A train of well dressed youths around her shone,
And every eye was fixed on her alone;
Her lively looks a sprightly mind disclose,
Quick as her eyes, and as unfixed as those:
Favors to none, to all she smiles extends;   25
Oft she rejects, but never once offends.
Bright as the sun her eyes the gazers strike,
And, like the sun, they shine on all alike.
Yet graceful ease, and sweetness void of pride,
Might hide her faults, if belles had faults to hide: 30
If to her share some female errors fall,
Look on her face, and you'll forgive them all.
   This nymph, to the destruction of mankind,
Nourished two locks, which graceful hung behind
In equal curls, and well conspired to deck   35
With shining ringlets her smooth ivory neck.
Love in these labyrinths his slaves detains,
And mighty hearts are held in slender chains.
With hairy sprindges we the birds betray,

Slight lines of hair surprise the finny prey,   40
Fair tresses man's imperial race ensnare,
And beauty draws us with a single hair.
   Th' adventrous Baron the bright locks admired,
He saw, he wished, and to the prize aspired:
Resolved to win, he meditates the way,   45
By force to ravish, or by fraud betray;
For when success a lover's toil attends,
Few ask, if fraud or force attained his ends.
   For this, ere Phoebus rose, he had implored
Propitious heaven, and every power adored,   50
But chiefly Love—to Love an altar built,
Of twelve vast French romances, neatly gilt.
There lay the sword-knot Sylvia's hands had sown,
With Flavia's busk that oft had rapped his own:
A fan, a garter, half a pair of gloves;   55
And all the trophies of his former loves.
With tender billet-doux he lights the pyre,
And breaths three amorous sighs to raise the fire.
Then prostrate falls, and begs with ardent eyes
Soon to obtain, and long possess the prize: 60
The powers gave ear, and granted half his prayer,
The rest, the winds dispersed in empty air.
   Close by those meads for ever crowned with flowers,
Where Thames with pride surveys his rising towers,
There stands a structure of majestic frame,   65
Which from the neighboring Hampton takes its name.
Here Britain's statesmen oft the fall foredoom
Of foreign tyrants, and of nymphs at home;
Here thou, great Anna! whom three realms obey,
Dost sometimes counsel take—and sometimes tea.   70
   Hither our nymphs and heroes did resort,
To taste awhile the pleasures of a court;
In various talk the cheerful hours they passed,
Of, who was bitt, or who capotted last:
This speaks the glory of the British Queen,   75
And that describes a charming Indian screen;
A third interprets motions, looks, and eyes;
At every word a reputation dies.
Snuff, or the fan, supply each pause of chat,
With singing, laughing, ogling, and all that.   80
   Now, when declining from the noon of day,
The sun obliquely shoots his burning ray;
When hungry judges soon the sentence sign,
And wretches hang that jury men may dine;

When merchants from th' Exchange return in peace,   85
And the long labors of the toilette cease—
The board's with cups and spoons, alternate, crowned;
The berries crackle, and the mill turns round;
On shining altars of Japan they raise
The silver lamp, and fiery spirits blaze;   90
From silver spouts the grateful liquors glide,
And China's earth receives the smoking tide;
At once they gratify their smell and taste,
While frequent cups prolong the rich repast.
Coffee (which makes the politician wise,   95
And see through all things with his half-shut eyes),
Sent up in vapors to the Baron's brain
New stratagems, the radiant lock to gain.
Ah cease rash youth! desist ere 'tis too late,
Fear the just gods, and think of Scylla's fate!   100
Changed to a bird, and sent to flit in air,
She dearly pays for Nisus' injured hair!
    But when to mischief mortals bend their mind,
How soon fit instruments of ill they find?
Just then, Clarissa drew with tempting grace   105
A two-edged weapon from her shining case;
So ladies in romance assist their knight,
Present the spear, and arm him for the fight.
He takes the gift with reverence, and extends
The little engine on his fingers' ends,   110
This just behind Belinda's neck he spread,
As o'er the fragrant steams she bends her head:
He first expands the glittering forfex wide
T'inclose the lock; then joins it, to divide;
One fatal stroke the sacred hair does sever   115
From the fair head, forever, and forever!
    The living fires come flashing from her eyes,
And screams of horror rend th' affrighted skies.
Not louder shrieks by dames to Heaven are cast,
When husbands die, or lap dogs breath their last,   120
Or when rich china vessels fallen from high,
In glittering dust and painted fragments lie!
    Let wreaths of triumph now my temples twine
(The victor cried), the glorious prize is mine!
While fish in streams, or birds delight in air,   125
Or in a coach and six the British fair,
As long as *Atalantis* shall be read,
Or the small pillow grace a lady's bed,
While visits shall be paid on solemn days,

When numerous wax-lights in bright order blaze,   130
While nymphs take treats, or assignations give,
So long my honor, name and praise shall live!
   What time would spare, from steel receives its date,
And monuments, like men, submit to fate!
Steel did the labor of the gods destroy,   135
And strike to dust th'aspiring towers of Troy;
Steel could the works of mortal pride confound,
And hew triumphal arches to the ground.
What wonder then, fair nymph! thy hairs should feel
The conquering force of unresisted steel?   140

Canto II

But anxious cares the pensive nymph oppressed,
And secret passions labored in her breast.
Not youthful kings in battle seized alive,
Not scornful virgins who their charms survive,
Not ardent lover robbed of all his bliss,   5
Not ancient lady when refused a kiss,
Not tyrants fierce that unrepenting die,
Not Cynthia when her manteau's pinned awry,
E'er felt such rage, resentment, and despair.
As thou, sad virgin! for thy ravished hair.   10
   While her racked soul repose and peace requires,
The fierce Thalestris fans the rising fires.
O wretched maid (she spreads her hands, and cried,
And Hampton's echoes, wretched maid! replied)
Was it for this you took such constant care,   15
Combs, bodkins, leads, pomatums, to prepare?
For this your locks in paper durance bound,
For this with torturing irons wreathed around?
Oh had the youth but been content to seize
Hairs less in sight—or any hairs but these!   20
Gods! shall the ravisher display this hair,
While the fops envy, and the ladies stare!
Honor forbid! at whose unrivaled shrine
Ease, pleasure, virtue, all, our sex resign.
Methinks already I your tears survey,   25
Already hear the horrid things they say,
Already see you a degraded toast,
And all your honor in a whisper lost!
How shall I, then, your helpless fame defend?
'Twill then be infamy to seem your friend!   30
And shall this prize, th' inestimable prize,
Exposed through crystal to the gazing eyes,
And heightened by the diamond's circling rays,
On that rapacious hand forever blaze?

Name _____

Date _____

Sooner shall grass in Hyde Park Circus grow,   35
And wits take lodgings in the sound of Bow;
Sooner let earth, air, sea, to chaos fall,
Men, monkeys, lap dogs, parrots, perish all!
   She said; then raging to Sir Plume repairs,
And bids her beau demand the precious hairs: 40
(Sir Plume, of amber snuffbox justly vain,
And the nice conduct of a clouded cane)
With earnest eyes, and round unthinking face,
He first the snuffbox opened, then the case,
And thus broke out—"My Lord, why, what the devil?   45
"Z—ds! d—the lock! 'fore Gad, you must be civil!
"Plague on't! 'tis past a jest—nay prithee, pox!
"Give her the hair"—he spoke, and rapped his box.
"It grieves me much" (replied the peer again)
"Who speaks so well should ever speak in vain.   50
But by this lock, this sacred lock I swear,
(Which never more shall join its parted hair,
Which never more its honors shall renew,
Clipped from the lovely head where once it grew)
That while my nostrils draw the vital air,   55
This hand, which won it, shall forever wear."
He spoke, and speaking in proud triumph spread
The long-contended honors of her head.
But see! the nymph in sorrow's pomp appears,
Her eyes half languishing, half drowned in tears;   60
Now livid pale her cheeks, now glowing red;
On her heaved bosom hung her drooping head,
Which, with a sigh, she raised; and thus she said,
"For ever cursed be this detested day,
Which snatched my best, my favorite curl away!   65
Happy! ah ten times happy, had I been,
If Hampton Court these eyes had never seen!
Yet am not I the first mistaken maid,
By love of courts to numerous ills betrayed.
Oh had I rather unadmired remained   70
In some lone isle, or distant northern land;
Where the gilt chariot never marked the way,
Where none learn ombre, none e'er taste bohea!
There kept my charms concealed from mortal eye,
Like roses that in deserts bloom and die.   75
What moved my mind with youthful lords to roam?
O had I stayed, and said my prayers at home!
'Twas this, the morning omens did fortell;
Thrice from my trembling hand the patchbox fell;
The tottering china shook without a wind,   80

227

Nay, Poll sat mute, and Shock was most unkind!
See the poor remnants of this slighted hair!
My hands shall rend what even thy own did spare.
This, in two sable ringlets taught to break,
Once gave new beauties to the snowy neck.   85
The sister lock now sits uncouth, alone,
And in its fellow's fate foresees its own;
Uncurled it hangs! the fatal shears demands;
And tempts once more thy sacrilegious hands."
She said: the pitying audience melt in tears,   90
But Fate and Jove had stopped the Baron's ears.
In vain Thalestris with reproach assails,
For who can move when fair Belinda fails?
Not half so fixed the Trojan could remain,
While Anna begged and Dido raged in vain.   95
To arms, to arms! the bold Thalestris cries,
And swift as lightning to the combat flies.
All side in parties, and begin th' attack;
Fans clap, silks rustle, and tough whalebones crack;
Heroes' and heroines' shouts confusedly rise,   100
And base, and treble voices strike the skies.
No common weapons in their hands are found,
Like gods they fight, nor dread a mortal wound.
   So when bold Homer makes the gods engage,
And heavenly breasts with human passions rage;   105
'Gainst Pallas, Mars, Latona, Hermes arms;
And all Olympus rings with loud alarms.
Jove's thunder roars, heaven trembles all around;
Blue Neptune storms, the bellowing deeps resound;
Earth shakes her nodding towers, the ground gives way, 110
And the pale ghosts start at the flash of day!
But trust the Muse—she saw it upward rise,
Though marked by none but quick poetic eyes:
(Thus Rome's great founder to the heavens withdrew,   170
To Proculus alone confessed in view.)
A sudden star, it shot through liquid air,
And drew behind a radiant trail of hair.
Not Berenice's locks first rose so bright,
The skies bespangling with disheveled light.   175
This, the beau monde shall from the mall survey,
As through the moonlight shade they nightly stray,
And hail with music its propitious ray.
This Partridge soon shall view in cloudless skies,
When next he looks through Galileo's eyes;   180
And hence th' egregious wizard shall foredoom
The fate of Louis, and the fall of Rome.

Then cease, bright nymph! to mourn the ravished hair
   Which adds new glory to the shining sphere!
Not all the tresses that fair head can boast   185
Shall draw such envy as the lock you lost.
For, after all the murders of your eye,
When, after millions slain, your self shall die;
When those fair suns shall set, as set they must,
And all those tresses shall be laid in dust;   190
This lock, the Muse shall consecrate to fame,
And midst the stars inscribe Belinda's name!

—Alexander Pope

Lesson 34
The Search for Collaboration

Objective

- To direct a meaningful use of secondary critical sources in a formal paper with a focus on poetry

Notes to the Teacher

The traditional high school research paper is often tacked onto the curriculum without question. The usual rationale for such an assignment is that it is important to familiarize college-bound students with the research form. This may be true. However, for this assignment to become a meaningful learning experience, it should be integrated as much as possible with other course work and not treated as an isolated activity. The study of poetry provides a variety of topics which lend themselves to manageable research. Likewise, guidelines for initiating and documenting research should be utilized in various ways before the formal research paper is assigned. (See *Research Paper*, a Center for Learning unit)

Procedures

1. Distribute **Handout 56.** Have students read the research paper and discuss its content. Ask some of the following questions:
   a. How is this paper different from critical papers you have written?
   b. Does the content of the paper agree with your understanding of the poem?
   c. What is the value of researching and writing such a paper?

2. Have students select a poet, period, literary movement or theme which interests them. This decision should be based on their recent literary experiences of primary sources. Sample topics include:
   a. Physical feminine beauty in the Renaissance: selections by Wyatt, Surrey, Petrarch, Spenser, Sidney and Shakespeare
   b. Punishment for sin in Dante and Milton
   c. Images of violence and death: select classical, medieval and renaissance examples
   d. Alienation in select poems by T. S. Eliot and Ezra Pound
   e. Mathematics and science in select metaphysical poems by John Donne
   f. Victorian attitudes in select poems by Tennyson, Arnold and Browning
   g. Friends remembered: Jonson's "To the Memory of My Beloved Master, William Shakespeare"; Milton's "Lycidas"; Wordsworth's "Elegaic Stanzas"; Auden's "In Memory of William Butler Yeats"
   h. Pre-Raphaelite "style" in Dante Gabriel Rosetti and select nineteenth century poets and painters
   i. The image of womanhood contrasted: select nineteenth and twentieth century examples
   j. The child is father of the man: Innocence in Blake, Gray, and Wordsworth
   k. Caricature as a satiric technique in Swift, Pope and Carrol
   l. Baroque sensibilities in the poetry of Richard Crashaw
   m. The therapeutic value of nature in romantic poetry: select examples
   n. Stoicism in the poetry of Emily Dickinson and Robert Frost
   o. Dew drops and roses in select cavalier poems
   p. Journey by Sea: Coleridge's "Ancient Mariner," Tennyson's "Ulysses" and Yeats' "Sailing to Byzantium"
   q. Classical mythology in renaissance poetry: select examples
   r. The role of Greek allusions in romantic poetry: Keats' "Ode on a Grecian Urn," Shelley's "Prometheus Unbound," Byron's "Prometheus," and Poe's "To Helen"

s. The sense of self pity in lyric poetry:
    select examples from Donne, Herrick,
    Shelley and Hopkins

t. Death and doom in select poems by
    Hardy and Housman

u. Color imagery in select poems by Wallace Stevens

v. Religious imagery in select cavalier
    poems by Robert Herrick, Richard
    Lovelace, and Andrew Marvell

w. Philosophical considerations in the
    poetry of Richard Wilbur

x. The democratic spirit in the poetry of
    Walt Whitman

y. Religious identity in select poems by
    Dickinson, Donne and Hopkins

z. Immortality through verse in select
    sonnets by Shakespeare

3. Help students limit their topics for treatment in a 1500-word paper.

4. Encourage students to explore available
    secondary resources which they will use
    for support for their theses.

5. As students become more familiar with
    their secondary sources, ask them to formulate a tentative thesis. As soon as this
    can be accomplished, students will be able
    to focus their gathering of information.

6. Give students directions for completing
    bibliography and note cards. Advise them
    to avoid the use of superficial sources such
    as encyclopaedias and study guides. Indicate the minimum number of secondary
    sources that they should utilize in their final papers. Indicate the need for various
    sources in order to allow for representative
    support for their ideas.

7. Give directions for the completion of the
    first and final drafts, including procedures
    for typing footnotes or endnotes, bibliography, etc.

8. Discuss the format of the paper (and any
    variations which you anticipate that
    would be different from that reflected on
    the handout).

An Analysis of Alexander Pope's
the Rape of the Lock

Alexander Pope's *The Rape of the Lock* has been described as a "complex mock-heroic—where Pope's urbane satire represents the culmination of a tradition of pseudo-epic poems in which the values and idiosyncrasies of an entire culture are satirized."[1] Some critics focus their analysis on Pope's poetic style—his use of rhythm, form, word choice, and poetic devices—parallelism, paradox, antithesis, juxtaposition, zeugma, irony, imagery, allusion, parody, metaphor, and symbolism. Others analyze Pope's poem with methods that are traditionally assigned to novels, such as character analysis, claiming that the characters reveal themselves through their thought, action, and speech. According to some critics, *The Rape of the Lock* does contain a moral, contrary to what other critics believe,[2] and this moral is revealed through a number of characters.

Pope's Style

Pope's technical craftsmanship cannot be questioned. Concerning *The Rape of the Lock*, Professor William Frost once remarked, "every poetic and logical energy is brought into focus, no syllable giving the effect of having been placed or selected at random."[3] Pope has been compared to Milton for his uncanny ability to vary the number and weight of stresses and pauses, and to mix run-on and end-stopped lines and couplets with extreme expressive skill.[4] While Pope varied the number of stresses, he usually retained the ten-syllable line.

In Pope's *Essay on Criticism*, he contends that the "sound must echo the sense." Pope, true to his own self-imposed rule, describes Belinda's 'toyshop of the heart,'

> Where Wigs with Wigs, with Sword-Knots Sword-Knots strive,
> Beaus banish Beaus, and Coaches Coaches drive.

"The repetitions of sounds collaborate with quick changes of syntax to suggest the clutter and chaos of Belinda's inner life."[5]

Pope also considered his audience when selecting his words. He appealed to readers and theatre-goers by using contemporary "types" of anatomized figures (prude, rake, coquette) and the latest language (wounds, charms, Ardors).[6]

The poem is written in heroic couplets (Pope's signature) because Pope "wished to emphasize by strong contrast...antithetic aspects of the truly 'epic' world and Belinda's pretentious world of petty social values."[7] These couplets are also "capable of achieving every known type of effect...high seriousness...low comedy...optimism...gloom...mirth...despair,"[8] in keeping with the mock-heroic form, Pope uses language ordinarily used to describe "the largest and best people, to describe small, bad people."[9]

Pope's Poetic Devices

Pope employs a variety of poetic devices in *The Rape of the Lock*. These include parallelism, paradox, antithesis, juxtaposition, zeugma, irony, imagery, parody, allusion, metaphor, and symbolism.

Parallelism, paradox, and antithesis are three very important, interrelated techniques that Pope uses to bind together the three worlds that run parallel to each other: the epic world; the world of social trivia; and the world of serious human issues.[10] Wherever there is a parallel, there is distinction, and wherever there is distinction, the possibility of a paradox, an antithesis, or at least a modulation.[11] Take the lines;

> Favours to none, to all she smiles extends,
> Oft she rejects, but never once offends.

The words Favours and smiles are parallel, not comparable, as they operate in different spheres. "None and all" are opposites, but comparable in the sense that they are equally objects of Belinda's detachment. "Oft and never" perform the same function as "none and all."[12]

The major antitheses are between the apparently frivolous subject and the heroic manner in which it is set forth, as well as between the serious human issues and the frivolous guise under which they are presented.[13]

The central paradox of the poem is also ironic—Belinda desires to retain her chastity, and yet she expects to and prepares to lose it.[14]

Pope uses juxtaposition either to reveal information without directly stating it or to achieve a link between contradictory aspects. The line, "Puffs, Powders, Patches, Bibles, Billet-doux," describes the confusion of the society world, epitomized in Belinda's untidy dressing table.[15] Pope compares Belinda to the sun, implying that she is a goddess, and therefore immortal. By juxtaposition, he reminds us:

> When those fair Suns shall sett, as sett they must,
> And all those Tresses shall be laid in Dust...

thus revealing Belinda's mortality.

The incongruity of *The Rape of the Lock* is essentially comic,[16] as is shown in the zeugma (the joining of two unlike objects, governed by a single verb) contained in these lines:

> Here Thou, Great Anna! whom three Realms obey,
> Dost sometimes Counsel take—and sometimes tea.

The incongruity shown here is the assumption that taking counsel and tea are of equal importance, which, of course, they are not.[17]

As stated before, the central paradox of the poem is also ironic. However, this is not the only type of irony present. Pope delighted in irony of false equation, as shown in the following passage from the revised version:[18]

> Whether the Nymph shall break Diana's Law,
> Or some frail China Jar receive a Flaw;
> Or stain her Honour, or her new Brocade;
> Forget her Pray'rs, or miss a Masquerade;
> Or lose her Heart, or Necklace, at a Ball;
> Or whether Heav'n has doom'd that Shock must fall

The irony lies in the distortion of viewpoint in the feminine mind that regards the cracking of a China vase or the staining of a new brocade as equivalent in seriousness to a violation of the double standard.[19]

The Rape of the Lock is also rich in imagery and periphrasis. "Verdant Field," "velvet plain," and "level Green" are all phrases that describe the card table. These phrases exhibit periphrasis, or circumlocutory diction, and they also conjure sensuous and unexpectedly fresh images.[20] In these expressions, the slightly enigmatic quality of epic language blends with lively sense impressions of scene, persons, and artifacts.[21]

The style of *The Rape of the Lock* is heroic—the invocation, the proposition of the subject, the descriptions, the moralizing asides, the speeches and the battle are practically the only structural features modeled on the epic.[22] Pope was not interested in ridiculing the epic, but rather in diminishing the affair of the lock of hair. Some critics believe that because Pope was translating the *Iliad* at the same time as he was writing *The Rape of the Lock*,[23] he used some *Iliad* events and speeches as bases for allusion and parody in his mock-epic poem.

The *Iliad* is not the only great work that Pope used as the basis for his allusions and parody. Ovid also influenced some major aspects of *The Rape of the Lock*. There are specific borrowings, such as the change of the lock into a star, the allusion to Scylla's theft of Nisus' sacred lock, and the comparison of Sir Fopling's death to "th' expiring Swan" of *Dido to Aeneas*.[24] The *Aeneid* also furnished some basis for allusion. Pope's lines;

> The hungry Judges soon the Sentence sign,
> And Wretches hang that Jury-men may Dine...

are a hideous corruption of these lines from Virgil's *Aeneid II;*[25]

> What time the judge forsakes the noisy bar
> To take repast, and stills the wordy war.

From the opening of the fourth *Aeneid,* the line, "But the Queen, long since wounded by anxious cares...is torn by secret passion," is the basis for these lines from *The Rape of the Lock:*[26]

> But anxious Cares the pensive Nymph oppest,
> And secret Passions labour'd in her Breast.

The dominant metaphor of *The Rape of the Lock* is the comparison of Belinda to the Sun. This metaphor is introduced early in the poem ("And op'd those Eyes which brighter shine than they").

Pope also uses symbolism in *The Rape of the Lock.* Two examples are: Belinda's chastity symbolized by her lock; and the game of ombre, which represents the war between the sexes.[27]

The Characters

The characters of *The Rape of the Lock* "make themselves appear ridiculous by their thought, speech, and actions... (within) a social microcosm...that is a simplified image of the real world."[28]

Belinda, the heroine of the poem, is seen in many different lights, not all of them harsh—as coquette, injured innocent, sweet charmer, society belle, rival of the sun, and murderer of millions.[29] This Cleopatra-like variety indicates simultaneously her charm, a vacuous lack of 'character,' the chameleon coquette's accomplishment as an actress, and also the peril of her position, dangerously 'unfix'd.'[30] Belinda is referred to in terms of beauty, purity, and even divinity: "the fair," "virgin," and "goddess." She moves in light as her natural element[31]—her ringlets are 'shining,' she herself is compared to the sun more than once, and called, "bright Nymph" and "the brightest Fair." However, Belinda does have a flaw—pride. Pride is Belinda's motive for her desire to remain seemingly inviolate and independent. She would therefore retain her maidenhood's power to domineer heartlessly over men.[32] The inscription of Belinda's name among the stars confirms in an unexpected way the importance the poem has half-jokingly ascribed to her.[33]

Clarissa sees through the vanity of the belle's domain, and she takes on the function of a chorus in the poem. She is a foil to the glittering 'toyshop of the Heart.'[34] She lacks Belinda's feminine divinity and sparkling manner, and reveals the moral of the poem.[35] Clarissa may be a catty old woman who enjoys the blow to a young beauty's vanity, or she may be the one who clearly knows that the lock and all it symbolizes must go if Belinda is ever to grow up.[36]

For 'Honour,' Thalestris would sacrifice 'Virtue' and everything else:

> Honour forbid! at whose unrival'd Shrine
> Ease, Pleasure, Virtue, All, our Sex resign.

"All" exposes the hollowness and muddle of her values; as a euphemism for virginity, it insinuates that reputation is worth more than chastity.[37] It would be unlikely for Thalestris to stand by Belinda should Belinda's 'Honour' be questioned—that would be 'Infamy.'

Because Pope could not be certain that the feud over Miss Arabella Fermor's cut lock (the real-life incident that inspired *The Rape of the Lock*) would end the chance of the marriage to the offender, Lord Petre, Pope could not afford to show the Baron (who represented Lord Petre) in too harsh a light. Pope purposely exploited the ambiguity of his mock epic to accomplish this task.

And the Moral of the Poem is...

The Rape of the Lock does not "deal in 'trifles without morals' "[38] as critic John Dennis contends. Pope once remarked to Joseph Spence, "that no poem was worth writing unless it contained a moral."[39] Pope's morality is finely interwoven into the mock-heroic structure of the poem.

For all of Pope's amused delight in the little world of society in *The Rape of the Lock*, he sees clearly that these ceremonies of manners are fatally flawed.[40] Thalestris' rebuke to Belinda,

> Gods! shall the ravisher display your hair,
> While the fops envy, and the ladies stare!
> Honour forbid! at whose unrival'd shrine
> Ease, Pleasure, Virtue, all, our sex resign.
> Methinks already I your tears survey,
> Already hear the horrid things they say,
> Already see you a degraded toast,
> And all your honour in a whisper lost!

shows that by mistaking social forms (the lock as a symbol of virginity and honor), for their meanings (actually being virginal and honorable), Thalestris not only distorts morals, but she also destroys manners.[41]

Conclusion

Although Edith Sitwell's comment that *The Rape of the Lock* was "fresh as the summer air blowing down the dew that tastes of the green leaves on which it has been lying"[42] may seem a bit vague and romantic in nature, the poem definitely is a technical and poetic masterpiece. Pope uses all the devices of a writer to create a work that is rich in language, characters, and morality.

237

Endnotes

[1]*Alexander Pope, Twentieth Century Interpretations of The Rape of the Lock*, ed. G. S. Rousseau (Englewood Cliffs, New Jersey: Prentice-Hall, Inc., 1969), 3.

[2]*Ibid.*, 12.

[3]*Ibid.*, 5.

[4]Douglas Bush, *English Poetry—The Main Currents from Chaucer to the Present* (New York: Oxford University Press, 1963), 85.

[5]Rousseau, Alexander Pope, 4.

[6]Ibid., 19.

[7]Ibid., 4.

[8]Ibid., 4.

[9]Thomas R. Edwards, *This Dark Estate: A Reading of Pope* (Los Angeles: University of California Press, 1963), 112.

[10]Rebecca Prince Parkin, *The Poetic Workmanship of Alexander Pope* (New York: Octagon Books, Inc., 1966), 74–75.

[11]Alexander Pope, *Pope—A Collection of Critical Essays*, ed. J. V. Guerinot (Englewood Cliffs, New Jersey: Prentice-Hall, Inc., 1972), 84.

[12]*Rousseau*, 5.

[13]Parkin, *The Poetic Workmanship*, 75.

[14]Ibid., 75.

[15]Rousseau, *Alexander Pope*, 5.

[16]Edwards, *This Dark Estate*, 98.

[17]Rousseau, *Alexander Pope*, 5.

[18]Parkin, *The Poetic Workmanship*, 45.

[19]Ibid., 46.

[20]Rousseau, *Alexander Pope*, 61.

[21]Ibid. 62

[22]Ibid. 39.

[23]Ibid., 60.

[24]Ibid., 58.

[25]Ibid., 71

[26]Ibid., 8.

[27]Parkin, *The Poetic Workmanship*, 17, 108.

[28]Rousseau, *Alexander Pope*, 3, 4.

[29]J. S. Cunningham, *Pope: The Rape of the Lock* (Woodbury, New York: Barron's Educational Series, Inc., 1961), 33.

[30]Ibid., 33.

[31]Ibid., 34.

[32]Rousseau, *Alexander Pope*, 73.

[33]Edwards, *This Dark Estate*, 21.

[34]Rousseau, *Alexander Pope*, 10.

[35]Ibid., 9.

[36]Ibid., 9–10.

[37]Cunningham, *Pope*, 46.

[38]Rousseau, *Alexander Pope*, 12.

[39]Ibid., 10–11.

[40]Edwards, *This Dark Estate*, 20.

[41]Ibid., 20.

[42]Edith Sitwell, *Alexander Pope* (New York: W. W. Norton & Company, Inc., 1962), 223.

Bibliography

Brooks, Cleanth. *The Well Wrought Urn—Studies in the Structure of Poetry.* New York: Harcourt, Brace & World, Inc., 1947.

Bush, Douglas. *English Poetry—The Main Currents from Chaucer to the Present.* New York: Oxford University Press, 1963.

Cunningham, J.S. *Pope: The Rape of the Lock.* Woodbury, New York: Barron's Educational Series, Inc., 1961.

Edwards, Thomas R. Jr. *This Dark Estate: A Reading of Pope.* Los Angeles: University of California Press, 1963.

Guerinot, J.V., ed. *Pope—A Collection of Critical Essays.* Englewood Cliffs, New Jersey: Prentice-Hall, Inc., 1972.

Hardy, J.P., *Reinterpretations—Essays on Poems by Milton, Pope, and Johnson.* London: Routledge & Kegan Paul, 1971.

Parkin, Rebecca Price. *The Poetic Workmanship of Alexander Pope.* New York: Octagon Books, Inc., 1966.

Rousseau, G.S., ed. *Twentieth Century Interpretations of the Rape of the Lock.* Englewood Cliffs, New Jersey: Prentice-Hall Inc., 1969.

Sitwell, Edith. *Alexander Pope.* New York: W.W. Norton & Company, Inc., 1962.

Index of Poems and Poets

Acknowledgments

For permission to reprint all works in this volume by each of the following authors, grateful acknowledgment is made to the holders of copyright, publishers, or representatives named below.

Lesson 1, Handout 1
Poem "Norman Morrison" by Adrian Mitchell from *Out Loud* by Adrian Mitchell. Copyright by W. H. Allen Publishers, London, England.

Lesson 1, Handout 1
"Norman Morrison" by David Ferguson from *Where Is Vietnam? American Poets Respond*, edited by Walter Lowenfels, with the assistance of Nan Braymer. Copyright 1967 by Walter Lowenfels, published by Anchor Books, a division of Doubleday & Company, Inc. Reprinted by permission of Manna Lowenfels, Literary Executrix.

Lesson 1, Handout 1
"Of Late" by George Starbuck from *White Paper* by George Starbuck. Copyright (c) 1965 by George Starbuck. First appeared in *Poetry Magazine.* By permission of Little, Brown and Company.

Lesson 1, Handout 1
"The Pacifists" from TIME, November 12, 1965. Copyright 1965 Time Inc. All rights reserved. Reprinted by permission from TIME.

Lesson 1, Handout 2
"Out, Out—" by Robert Frost. Copyright 1916 by Holt, Rinehart and Winston and renewed 1944 by Robert Frost. Reprinted from *The Poetry Of Robert Frost* edited by Edward Connery Lathem, by permission of Henry Holt and Company, Inc.

Lesson 2, Handout 4
"Last Speech to the Court" by Bartolomeo Vanzetti from *The Letters Of Sacco And Vanzetti*, ed. Marion Denman Frankfuter and Gardner Jackson, Copyright 1928 by The Viking Press, Inc. Copyrights renewed 1955 by The Viking Press, Inc. All rights reserved. Reprinted by permission of Viking Penguin, Inc.

Lesson 2, Handout 4
"Justice Denied in Massachusetts" by Edna St. Vincent Millay from *Renascence and other Poems* (reprinted by Norma Millay Ellis). Published 1941 by Harper and Brothers, New York.

Lesson 3, Handout 6
"Daddy" and "Happy Father's Day" by William P. Middleton, Pittsburgh, PA. Unpublished manuscript.

Lesson 3, Handout 7
"Daddy" from *Ariel* by Sylvia Plath. Copyright (c) 1963 by Ted Hughes. Reprinted by permission of Harper & Row, Publishers, Inc.

Lesson 4, Handout 10
"Nobody Comes" by Thomas Hardy. Reprinted with permission of Macmillan Publishing Company from *The Complete Poems of Thomas Hardy*, edited by James Gibson. Copyright 1925 by Macmillan Publishing Company, renewed 1953 by Lloyds Bank Ltd.

Lesson 5, Handout 12
"Ode On A Grecian Urn" by John Keats from *English And Western Literature*. Published 1984 by Macmillan Publishing Co., New York, New York.

Lesson 6, Handout 13
"Ode To Ben Jonson" by Robert Herrick from *English and Western Literature*. Published 1984 by Macmillan Publishing Co., New York, New York.

Lesson 6, Handout 14
"Sound And Sense" by Alexander Pope from *Sound And Sense: An Introduction to Poetry*, Laurence Perring, Editor. Published 1973 by Harcourt Brace Jovanovich, New York.

Lesson 6, Handout 14
"Player Piano" by John Updike. Copyright (c) 1954 by John Updike. Reprinted from *The Carpentered Hen And Other Tame Creatures* by John Updike, by permission of Alfred A. Knopf, Inc.

Lesson 6, Handout 14
"Preface to a Poetry Reading" by Samuel Hazo from *Nightwords* (Sheep Meadows Press, 1988). Reprinted with permission.

Lesson 6,
"A Fit Of Rhyme Against Rhyme" by Ben Jonson from *Poems For Study*, Leonard Unger, 1953. Published by Rinehart & Co.

Lesson 7, Handout 15
Lyrics to song "I Am A Rock" by Paul Simon. Copyright © 1965 Paul Simon.

Lesson 7, Handout 15
Lyrics to song "The Promised Land" by Bruce Springsteen which was taken from album, *Darkness On The Edge of Town*, 1978, Columbia Records, Terre Haute, Indiana.

Lesson 9, Handout 20
"A Lecture Upon The Shadow" by John Donne from *Adventures In World Literature*, 1970. Published by Harcourt Brace Jovanovich, New York.

Lesson 10, Handout 22
"If We Must Die..." by Claude McKay from *Selected Poems*. Copyright (c) 1981 and reprinted with the permission of Twayne Publishers, a division of G. K. Hall & Co., Boston.

Lesson 11, Handout 24
"On The Late Massacre In Piedmont" by John Milton from *Poems For Study*, Leonard Unger, 1953. Published by Rinehart & Company.

Lesson 11, Handout 24
"The Destruction of Sennacherib" by George Gordon, Lord Byron from *Western Wind* by John Frederick Nims, 1974. Published by Random House, New York.

Lesson 12, Handout 26
"I Know I'm Not Sufficiently Obscure" by Ray Durem from *Take No Prisoners*. Published 1971 by Paul Breman Publishers, Ltd., London, England.

Lesson 13, Handout 27
"No Images" by Waring Cuney from *The Book Of American Negro Poetry* by James Weldon Johnson, copyright (c) 1931 by Harcourt Brace Jovanovich, Inc. and renewed 1959 by Grace Nail Johnson, reprinted by permission of the publisher.

Lesson 13, Handout 28
"Root Cellar" by Theodore Roethke. Copyright 1943 by Modern Poetry Association, Inc. From *The Collected Poems Of Theodore Roethke*. Reprinted by permission of Doubleday, Dell Publishing Group, Inc.

Lesson 14, Handout 29
"Very Like A Whale" by Ogden Nash from *Verses From 1929 On* by Ogden Nash. Copyright 1934 by The Curtis Publishing Co. By permission of Little, Brown and Company, Boston, Massachusetts.

Lesson 15, Handout 30
"when serpents bargain for the right to squirm" is reprinted from COMPLETE POEMS, 1913–1962 by E. E. Cummings, by permission of Liveright Publ. Corp. Copyright © 1923, 1925, 1931, 1935, 1938, 1939, 1940, 1944, 1945, 1946, 1947, 1948, 1949, 1950, 1951, 1952, 1953, 1954, 1955, 1956, 1957, 1958, 1959, 1960, 1961, 1962 by the Trustees for the E. E. Cummings Trust. Copyright © 1961, 1963, 1968 by Marion Morehouse Cummings.

Lesson 15, Handout 30
"The Emperor of Ice Cream" by Wallace Stevens. Copyright 1923 and renewed 1951 by Wallace Stevens. Reprinted from *The Collected Poems Of Wallace Stevens*, by permission of Alfred A. Knopf, Inc.

Lesson 16, Handout 32
"Hope" by George Herbert from *Western Wind*, John Frederick Nims, Editor. Published by Random House, New York, 1974.

Lesson 16, 23, Handout 32, 41
"Hope Is The Thing With Feathers" and "I Died For Beauty" by Emily Dickinson. Reprinted by permission of the publishers and the Trustees of Amherst College from *The Poems Of Emily Dickinson*, Edited by Thomas H. Johnson, Cambridge, Mass.: The

Belknap Press of Harvard University Press, Copyright 1951, (c) 1955, 1979, 1983 by The President and Fellows of Harvard College.

Lesson 17, Handout 33
"The Wayfarer" by Stephen Crane from *Poems*, 4th Edition by C. F. Main and P. J. Seng, Editors, 1978. Published by Wadsworth Publishing Company, Belmont, California.

Lesson 17, Handout 33
"Many Workmen" by Stephen Crane from *Poems*, 4th Edition by C. F. Main and P. J. Seng, Editors, 1978. Published by Wadsworth Publishing Company, Belmont, California.

Lesson 17, Handout 33
"The World" by Henry Vaughan from *Poems For Study*, by Leonard Unger, 1953. Published by Rinehart & Company.

Lesson 18, Handout 34
"Naming Of Parts" from *A Map Of Verona* by Henry Reed, 1973. Copyright by the Estate of Henry Reed. Published by Jonathan Cape Ltd., London, England. Reprinted with permission.

Lesson 18, Handout 34
"Spring" by Gerard Manley Hopkins from *Sound And Sense: An Introduction to Poetry*, Laurence Perrine, 1973. Published by Harcourt Brace Jovanovich, New York.

Lesson 19, Handout 35
Excerpts from "Song Of Myself" by Walt Whitman from *Whitman*, Leslie Fiedler, Editor, 1959. Published by Laurel/Dell Publishing, New York, New York.

Lesson 22, Handout 40
"In Westminster Abbey" by John Betjeman from *Collected Poems*. Published by John Murray Publishers, Ltd., London, England.

Lesson 22, Handout 40
"La Belle Dame Sans Merci" by John Keats from *A World Elsewhere: Romance*, Jewkes and Frye, Editors, 1973. Published by Harcourt Brace Jovanovich, New York.

Lesson 24, Handout 43
"Patterns" from *The Complete Poetical Works of Amy Lowell* by Amy Lowell. Copyright (c) 1955 by Houghton Mifflin Company. Copyright (c) 1983 renewed by Houghton Mifflin Company, Brinton P. Roberts, Esquire and G. D'Andelot Helin, Esquire. Reprinted by permission of Houghton Mifflin Company.

Lesson 24, Handout 43
Lyrics to song "Patterns" by Paul Simon. Copyright © 1965 Paul Simon.

Language Arts Series

Advanced Placement
Advanced Placement English: Practical Approaches to Literary Analysis
Advanced Placement English: In-depth Analysis of Literary Forms
Advanced Placement Poetry
Advanced Placement Short Story
Advanced Placement Writing 1
Advanced Placement Writing 2

Composition
Advanced Composition
Advanced Composition, Student Edition
Basic Composition
Basic Composition, Student Edition
Creative Writing
Daily Writing Topics
Formula Writing 1—Building Toward Writing Proficiency
Formula Writing 2—Diverse Writing Situations
Grammar Mastery—For Better Writing, Workbook Level 1
Grammar Mastery—For Better Writing, Workbook Level 2
Grammar Mastery—For Better Writing, Teacher Guide
Journalism: Writing for Publication
Research 1: Information Literacy
Research 2: The Research Paper
Writing 1: Learning the Process
Writing 2: Personalizing the Process
Writing Skills and the Job Search

Genres
Creative Dramatics in the Classroom
Mythology
Nonfiction: A Critical Approach
Participating in the Poem
Science Fiction—19th Century
Short Poems: Their Vitality and Versatility
The Short Story

Literary Traditions
American Literature 1: Beginnings through Civil War
American Literature 2: Civil War to Present
Archetypes in Life, Literature, and Myth of Reason
British Literature 1: Beginnings to Age
British Literature 2: Romantics to the Present
Honors American Literature 1
Honors American Literature 2
Multicultural Literature: Essays, Fiction, and Poetry
World Literature 1
World Literature 2

Skills
Junior High Language Arts
Speech
Thinking, Reading, Writing, Speaking

Special Topic
Supervisor/Student Teacher Manual
Peer Mediation: Training Students in Conflict Resolution

The Publisher

All instructional materials identified by the TAP® (Teachers/Authors/Publishers) trademark are developed by a national network of teachers whose collective educational experience distinguishes the publishing objective of The Center for Learning, a non-profit educational corporation founded in 1970.

Concentrating on values-related disciplines, The Center publishes humanities and religion curriculum units for use in public and private schools and other educational settings. Over 500 language arts, social studies, novel/drama, life issues, and faith publications are available.

While acutely aware of the challenges and uncertain solutions to growing educational problems, The Center is committed to quality curriculum development and to the expansion of learning opportunities for all students. Publications are regularly evaluated and updated to meet the changing and diverse needs of teachers and students. Teachers may offer suggestions for development of new publications or revisions of existing titles by contacting

The Center for Learning

Administrative/Editorial Office
21590 Center Ridge Road
Rocky River, Ohio, 44116
(440) 331-1404 • FAX (440) 331-5414
E-mail: cfl@stratos.net
Web: http://www.centerforlearning.org

For a free catalog, containing order and price information, and a descriptive listing of titles, contact

The Center for Learning

Shipping/Business Office
P.O. Box 910
Villa Maria, PA 16155
(412) 964-8083 • (800) 767-9090
FAX (888) 767-8080